Student's Guide

to accompany

Abnormal Psychology and Modern Life

SEVENTH EDITION

Student's Guide
to accompany

Abnormal Psychology and Modern Life

SEVENTH EDITION

Coleman   Butcher   Carson

Prepared by

Mary P. Koss
Kent State University

Scott, Foresman and Company

Glenview, Illinois   Dallas, Tex.   Oakland, N.J.
Palo Alto, Cal.   Tucker, Ga.   London, England

ISBN 0-673-15887-X

2   3   4   5   6-DBH-89   88   87   86   85   84

Contents

Preface

In most schools abnormal psychology is one of the most popular psychology courses offered. Commonly, there are students enrolled in this course whose major fields are quite diverse and who have taken only an introductory course in psychology. These students sometimes feel at a disadvantage competing with upper-level psychology majors. In addition, abnormal psychology can be a tricky subject area. The familiarity of the subject matter and its high relevance to real life may give some students the feeling that they "understand" the material only to find out at examination time that they do not "know" the material the way the instructor expected.

This study guide has been developed to assist you in learning the material presented in the textbook. It has been designed to help you overcome any lack of experience you may have in approaching psychological material and to make you familiar with the kind of information you should really know in order to do well on exams. It is written in a straightforward and serious style, minimizing games and other gimmicks. Most students find the textbook, *Abnormal Psychology and Modern Life,* contains so many case histories and examples that they become interested in and motivated to learn the material without any outside props. What students *do* need is help with deciding what to learn since the textbook is quite detailed. The goal of this study guide is to show you what to learn and to provide you with a place to write down the information to be learned so you will have notes to use in studying for examinations.

HOW TO STUDY

Many teachers recommend the following approach to studying course material:
1. Skim major headings and read chapter summary.
2. Read and highlight (underline) important sections of the text.
3. Outline the important points you have highlighted in your reading. (Psychological studies show that putting material into your own words helps you to learn and retain it better.)
4. Study from your text notes and class notes for exams—not from your textbook. Start studying a few days in advance. (Studying from your underlined text is confusing, not as effective, and may make you feel more anxious and unprepared.)

This study guide has been written as a check on the appropriateness of your Stage 2 reading. It indicates the terms and concepts many teachers feel are most important in the text. Do you seem to be underlining the same points? If not, the guide will help you pick up on points you have overlooked rather than have you wait until exam time for this feedback. The most important function of the study guide, however, is as a substitute for the difficult and time-consuming outlining recommended in Stage 3. In the study guide, you will find that a lot of the choosing and organizing of the material has been done for you. Also, whenever possible, the charts have been constructed to help you consolidate and learn the material. You have been given the general outlines. Your job is to fill in the specific information so you end up with a complete and efficient set of notes to use in studying for examinations.

HOW TO USE THIS STUDY GUIDE

The study guide follows the sequence of the textbook and uses the same chapter headings and section headings. Each study guide chapter consists of four sections.

1. Chapter overview

This short section is designed to prepare you to begin the chapter. Rather than just summarizing what the chapter is about (the text chapter summaries do this), the overview is designed to orient you to the purpose and some of the implications of the material you are about to read. It is designed to alert you to the overall importance of the chapter so you will, hopefully, feel motivated to start reading it. It is recommended that you first read the overview, then read the chapter summary in the textbook. Next skim the chapter by reading the major section headings so you get a mental picture of the overall organization of the chapter. Now go back to the beginning of the chapter and begin reading and highlighting the text. After you have done this, you are ready to begin filling in the study guide sections.

2. Terms you should know

Here you will find listed all the major terms introduced in the chapter along with a page reference on which to find the definition of the term in the textbook. To assist your locating the terms, care has been taken to ensure that they are listed in exactly the same form or wording as in the textbook. Many of the terms can also be found in the glossary at the back of the textbook. However, it is still a good idea to look up the definition of the term within the chapter to be certain you know the context in which the term appeared. In the space provided, write out a brief definition of each term.

3. Concepts to master

Each major section heading in the text is treated as a concept and is numbered consecutively. Under each numbered concept are specific points of information identified by small letters. Each requires that you provide some information. You may have to write a short answer, complete a chart, match two columns, or fill in blanks. The page reference tells you where to find the requested information. The language of the questions parallels as much as possible that used in the textbook to make it easier for you to locate the answer in your book.

The concepts have been chosen so that you have a guide to the most important topics in the chapter. The specific questions help you identify the factual knowledge you should learn about each topic. To complete the requested information, go to the referenced page, locate the appropriate section and read it over, then write a correct response in your own words in the study guide. As much space as possible has been provided for you to write in your answers, but in some cases you may have to continue on a separate page. Answer the questions carefully, completely, and accurately, and you will end up with a detailed outline of each chapter that you can use instead of the textbook to study efficiently for examinations.

At the end of the concepts section, you will notice that there are some concepts whose numbers are in parentheses. This indicates that this concept is based on one of the text's highlights. Many instructors assign these highlights optionally. Therefore, they have been placed together at the end of the concept section so you can easily skip them if your teacher won't be using them.

4. Self-test

Each study guide chapter concludes with a short self-test of multiple-choice items. The self-test will not only allow you to assess your mastery of the chapter, it will allow you to get a feeling for some of the types of questions that may appear on your course examinations. Complete the self-test items after you have completed the study guide terms and concepts sections and after you are about halfway into your studying for the examination. Look up the correct answer to each item. Go back to the referenced page for each item you missed and read over the correct answer. Then try to analyze why you made the mistake. Did you not know the material? (Try to study more.) Did you misinterpret the item? (Try to read each item very carefully and make sure you know the definitions of all the terms introduced in the chapter. During tests remember you can usually ask your instructor to define a word you don't know as long as it is not a technical term you were supposed to learn.)

HOW TO PREPARE FOR EXAMS

Many students become anxious about their performance on tests and this tension becomes increasingly greater as the exam time becomes nearer. Research suggests that the most effective preparation is accomplished under moderate levels of anxiety. Therefore, do not leave all your studying until the last minute when tension renders your behavior disorganized and less effective. Read the text and complete the study guide on an ongoing basis during the term, and aim to complete these tasks several days before the exam.

Plan to study for a few hours each day on the several days before the scheduled exam. Study from your completed study guide and your class notes, not from your textbook. Re-reading the textbook is time consuming and inefficient. If you've been conscientious in completing the study guide, it contains the material you need to learn. Start with the "Terms You Should Know" section. Cover the definition and try to recite it from memory. (If you have a private study area, it's even more effective to say the definition out loud.) Go back over the list and cover each term successively. Read the definition and try to recall the term to which it applies. This general approach is to be used with the "Concepts to Master" section as well. Cover the answers you have written and try to generate them from memory. Continue to review the study guide until you can reproduce all the correct answers from memory.

Whether your teacher will be using multiple-choice or essay exams doesn't affect how you will prepare—both types of testing require a command of the basic facts. Good, well-prepared students come out on top no matter what form of testing the instructor uses. Some students may argue that memorization isn't necessary for multiple-choice tests which only require recognition of the right response. This is untrue. Instructors purposely write the wrong answers to look and sound plausible. If you don't know the facts, you'll be misled by these distractors.

CONCLUSION

I've been a teacher of abnormal psychology for ten years. The suggestions I have made and the way I've set up this study guide reflect an approach that has helped many of my students. I hope the guide helps you build a good foundation of knowledge about abnormal behavior that you can add to in years to come through your personal experiences, reading, and new scientific developments you become aware of through the media.

Good luck,
Mary P. Koss

1

Abnormal behavior in our times

OVERVIEW

It has been said that psychology "has a long history but a short past." This is certainly true of abnormal psychology. Although examples of bizarre behavior are seen throughout history, and considerations of why people act as they do have appeared and reappeared in literature and philosophy, scientific study of abnormal behavior really only began around 1900. Consequently, it is not surprising that many misconceptions about mentally ill people still exist. Chapter 1 discusses some of the misconceptions held by many people. An appreciation for the value of scientific data coupled with awareness of the limitations of research studies is the best way to correct these misconceptions.

Then the whole issue of labeling is presented. Labeling a person's behavior as "abnormal" is sometimes harmful and is often influenced by the values of the labeler. The difficulty of differentiating "normal" from "abnormal" is discussed in Chapter 1, and the categories officially considered abnormal by psychiatrists are presented.

TERMS YOU SHOULD KNOW

abnormal psychology (p. 14)

clinical psychology (p. 15)

psychiatry (p. 15)

social work (p. 15)

psychopathology (p. 15)

abnormal (p. 15)

reliability (p. 16)

validity (p. 16)

CONCEPTS TO MASTER

1. The age of anxiety
   The authors note that the present times are characterized by a large number of anxious, unhappy, bewildered people.
   a. What are some of the characteristics of our society that lead to these feelings? (pp. 5–6)

   b. Certain human behaviors "reveal" the stress of our times. For example,
      1. How many people are affected by mental disorders compared to the number of people affected by physical disorders? (p. 6)

      treatment   1 in 7 people will receive
      20% have diagnosible mental illness

2

2. President Carter's Commission on Mental Health concluded that eventually one person in _____7_____ requires professional treatment for emotional disorders. (p. 6)

2. Popular views of abnormal behavior
   a. What is the major point about abnormal behavior that is illustrated by the many examples obtained from historical documents which the authors present? (p. 7)

   b. How is literature valuable to the person interested in abnormal behavior? (pp. 9–10)

3. Some popular misconceptions
   a. How has the misconception that abnormal behavior is always bizarre come about? (p. 10)

   b. The authors indicate that no sharp dividing line exists between "normal" and "abnormal." The drawing below indicates the "continuum of behavior" from normal to abnormal. Which of the following statements are true about it? Circle the correct response. (pp. 11–12)
      1. The behavior of different individuals ranges by imperceptible degrees from normal to abnormal. True False
      2. From time to time individuals shift their place along the continuum. True False
      3. All behavior is an attempt to cope with life's problems as the individual perceives them. True False

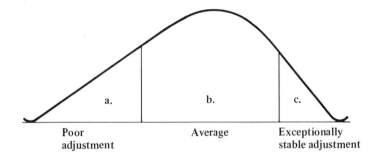

Poor adjustment   Average   Exceptionally stable adjustment

   c. The view that former mental patients are dangerous is not completely accurate. (pp. 12–13)
      1. How does the arrest rate of former patients compare to the general population? (p. 12)

      2. Overall, what percentage of former mental patients can be regarded as dangerous to themselves or others? (p. 13)

   d. According to the text, are the mentally disordered more likely to make literary and artistic contributions to society? (p. 14)

e. The fact that anxiety over one's mental status is a universal fear is demonstrated by the finding that one person in _____ responded yes when asked in a survey if he or she had ever felt he or she was going to have a "nervous breakdown." (p. 14)

4. Abnormal behavior as the scientist sees it
   a. What is the literal meaning of the word *abnormal*? (p. 15)

   b. What is the "cultural relativist" view of abnormal behavior as described by Ullman and Krasner? (p. 15)

   What are the two serious problems, mentioned in the text, with this viewpoint? (p. 15)

   c. Describe the view of abnormal behavior, "abnormal as maladaptive," adopted in the text. (pp. 15–16)

   d. What are the two assumptions on which this view rests? (p. 16)

   How do the authors justify considering prejudice, discrimination, waste of natural resources, and polluting the environment to be "abnormal behavior"? (p. 16)

   e. What is the advantage of the term *maladaptive* over the term *abnormal?* (p. 16)

   f. What do the authors say about the goal of therapy within an "abnormal-behavior-as-maladaptive-behavior" framework? (p. 16)

5. The problem of classification
   a. What is a "classification" in abnormal psychology used for? (p. 16)

   b. To what extent has psychology been able to develop a reliable and valid classification system? (p. 16)

4

c. Regarding the Diagnostic and Statistical Manual of Mental Disorders (DSM–III):
   1. A distinct feature of DSM–III is "operational criteria." What does this mean? What is the result of the use of strict criteria? (p. 17)

   2. Identify the five axes of DSM–III: (pp. 17–18)
      Axis I

      Axis II

      Axis III

      Axis IV

      Axis V.

   3. Axis I and II list the mental disorders.
      Place the following terms under their appropriate headings: mental retardation, alcohol abuse, psychosomatic disorders, severe depression, Alzheimer's disease, schizophrenia, autism, and anxiety disorders. (p. 18)

Category	Examples
organic mental disorders	
substance use disorders	
disorders of psychological or sociocultural origin	
disorders arising during childhood or adolescence	

4. Why do some clinicians object to the use of Axes IV and V on insurance forms?   (p. 19)

5. The authors list two limitations of DSM–III. Explain each: (pp. 19–20)
   a. DSM–III just describes things.

   b. DSM–III only covers individual behavior.

6. The authors of the text indicate that the process of labeling, no matter what classification system is used, has drawbacks.   (pp. 21–22)
   a. First, what are two ways labels may affect persons who work with mentally disordered persons?

   b. Second, how might labels affect the patients themselves?

6. Research in abnormal psychology
   a. Abnormal behavior shares with the rest of psychology a focus on _____.
   However, self-observation as a form of behavior has two major limitations: (p. 22)
   1.
   2.
   How are inferences used to make sense of observed abnormal behavior?   (p. 23)

   b. Research in abnormal psychology is concerned with gaining enhanced
   _____ and if possible _____ of abnormal
   behavior. One strategy of research is the single case study, the major limitation of which is that we
   can't know for sure if observed characteristics are related to the disorder, to unique characteristics of the subject, to characteristics of the _____ or an interaction.
   To overcome these limitations, a representative _____ is usually
   studied rather than single cases and often both a group of people with the disorder (the
   experimental group) and a group of comparable people who do not have the disorder (the
   _____ group) are studied.   (pp. 23–24)

c. Criminals come from broken homes much more frequently than noncriminals. Therefore, why can't we assume that broken homes cause crime? (p. 25)

d. Match the following terms and definitions.

Term	Definition
1. retrospective research	a. Therapist intensively studies a client's background.
2. waiting list control	b. Mathematical corrections are made for uncontrolled group differences.
3. case study method	c. Subjects studied over an extended period.
4. experimental method	d. Treatment is withheld for a period of time.
5. statistical control	e. All factors are controlled except for the one of interest.
6. longitudinal study	f. Subjects are asked to recall their childhood experiences.

e. Describe the strengths and limitations of each of the following methods. (pp. 26–27)

experimental method	1. Can determine cause and effect relationships.	1. Impractical and unethical in abnormal psychological research.
case study method	1. Sometimes results in useful insights.	1.
retrospective research	1. Standard method of clinical inquiry.	1. Hard to disentangle cause and effect. 2. Disordered person may not be accurate. 3.
prospective studies	1. Cause and effect can be determined with greater confidence than in retrospective studies.	1. Hard to get a large number of disordered subjects unless a "high risk" strategy is used. 2. 3. 4.

7

7. Orientation of the book (pp. 27–28)
   a. What is involved in a "scientific approach"? (p. 27)

   What does it mean to "take a critical and evaluative attitude toward research findings"? (p. 27)

   b. How can a student develop an awareness of "common human concerns?" (pp. 27–28)

   c. How do the authors of the text view mentally disordered persons in order to respect their dignity? (p. 28)

(8.) Estimated prevalance of major maladaptive behavior patterns in the United States
   a. Assuming a population of 220 million, approximately 1 person in _____ suffers from minor emotional problems such as "demoralization" while 1 person in _____ experiences serious problems such as schizophrenia. (p. 7)
   b. Define the following terms: (p. 29)
      1. incidence

      2. prevalance.

(9.) Patients in mental hospitals
   a. What has happened to the number of persons confined to state and county mental hospitals over the last 20 years? (p. 12)

   b. What are the five reasons mentioned in the text that account for the above changes? (p. 12)

(10.) Mental illness as a myth
   a.   Describe Szasz's view of mental illness.

   b.   What do Sarbin and Mancuso (1980) mean when they say that schizophrenia is a "moral verdict"?

CHAPTER QUIZ

1.   Which of the following statements regarding the age of anxiety is true?
   a.   Mental impairments affect almost as many people as physical problems.
   b.   One person in 20 will eventually require help for emotional problems.
   c.   Emotional factors are acknowledged to have widespread influence on purely physical diseases.
   d.   According to the authors of the text, the typical college student has many reasons to have grand hopes for the future.
2.   Which of the following statements is a misconception about mental disorders?
   a.   Most hospitalized patients are quite aware of what goes on around them.
   b.   The majority of cases of "mental illness" are simply self-defeating and maladaptive behavior.
   c.   From time to time most people behave somewhat abnormally.
   d.   People who might today be diagnosed as having a mental disorder made the bulk of artistic and literary contributions in former times.
3.   Compared to the dangerousness of the general population, former mental patients
   a.   are no more likely to be arrested than anyone else.
   b.   are regarded as dangerous in only 5 percent of cases.
   c.   do engage in violent acts especially if they have suffered a very serious mental disorder.
   d.   may be violent if they had a history of dangerousness prior to their mental illness.
4.   The professional psychological specialty concerned with the study, assessment, and treatment of abnormal behavior is
   a.   abnormal psychology.
   b.   clinical psychology.
   c.   psychiatry.
   d.   social work.
5.   The word *abnormal* literally means behavior that
   a.   deviates from society's norms.
   b.   interferes with the well-being of the individual.
   c.   is "away from the normal."
   d.   is undesirable.
6.   The authors of the textbook maintain that the best criteria for determining the normality of behavior is
   a.   deviance from the norm.
   b.   adaptivity of the behavior in furthering individual and group well-being.
   c.   variance from societal expectations.
   d.   the operational criteria listed in the DSM–III.
7.   Which of the following statements regarding psychiatric classification is *incorrect*?
   a.   Classification involves defining various categories of maladaptive behavior.
   b.   Classification is a first step in research and treatment of mental disorders.
   c.   A reliable classification system tells something important about the entity classified.
   d.   Classification systems are fundamentally arbitrary.

8. The DSM–III's operational definitions of mental disorders has led to
   a. much more behavior being assigned to wastebasket categories.
   b. an increased validity of diagnoses.
   c. reduced reliability in the application of diagnostic labels.
   d. increases in the subjective elements in the diagnostic process.
9. Many clinicians object to the inclusion of an axis _____ diagnosis on insurance forms because it violates the client's confidentiality.
   a. Axis I
   b. Axis II
   c. Axis III
   d. Axis IV.
10. DSM–III's major categories of mental disorders include
   a. organic mental disorders.
   b. schizophrenic disorders.
   c. adjustment disorders.
   d. psychosexual disorders.
11. Which of the following terms refers to a mental condition of relatively short duration?
   a. episodic
   b. acute
   c. chronic
   d. factitious.
12. All of the following are major criticisms of the use of DSM–III labels except:
   a. the labels name, they do not explain.
   b. labels may affect the expectations of the treatment staff.
   c. labels may influence the treatment a client receives.
   d. labels only encourage further study of the client.
13. In psychological research, a group which exhibits the disorder of interest is called a
   a. representative sample.
   b. experimental group.
   c. waiting list control.
   d. statistical control.
14. Rapists were found to come from homes where a father was absent in 80 percent of the cases whereas nonsex offenders were found to come from such homes in 20 percent of cases. We may confidently assume that
   a. father absence causes rape.
   b. both sexual and nonsexual crimes are caused by father absence.
   c. father absence is significantly associated with rape.
   d. no conclusion can be reached from the data given.
15. Assume a scientist set out to examine yearly all children born that year at a local hospital to schizophrenic mothers. Which of the following terms describing psychological methods *does not* apply to this study?
   a. prospective research
   b. longitudinal design
   c. case study method
   d. high risk study.

2
Historical views of abnormal behavior

OVERVIEW

Abnormal behavior has fascinated humankind from its beginning, and various explanations of the cause of such behavior have been developed over the course of history. It's important to know what a particular group of people thought about the cause of bizarre behavior, since beliefs usually predict the way people treat mentally ill people.

There are basically four models for understanding abnormal behavior: demonological, biological, psychosocial, and sociocultural. The first two have roots in ancient times; the latter two are more recent inventions.

An understanding of the older viewpoints presented in this chapter helps in understanding why scientists working at the beginning of this century believed there was the need for drastic changes in thinking.

TERMS YOU SHOULD KNOW

trephining (p. 32)

exorcism (p. 33)

tarantism (p. 37)

lycanthropy (p. 37)

moral therapy (p. 49)

general paresis (p. 52)

11

CONCEPTS TO MASTER

1. Abnormal behavior in ancient times (up to A.D. 500)
    a. How were mental disorders treated by Stone Age cave dwellers? (p. 32)

    Would you consider this treatment humane or cruel? (p. 32)

    b. Hippocrates, the "father of modern medicine," is credited in your text with five important ideas that contributed to the development of abnormal psychology. What were these? (pp. 33–34)

    How did Hippocrates believe mental and physical diseases were caused? (p. 34)

    c. Plato is credited with originating ideas with relevance to the legal status of the insane and community treatment of the mentally disordered. What were his ideas? (p. 34)

    d. Match the following names with their major contributions: (p. 35)

Name	Major Contribution
1. Aristotle (384–322 B.C.)	a. Advanced knowledge of the anatomy of the nervous system.
2. Asclepiades (ca. 124 B.C.)	
3. Cicero (106–43 B.C.)	b. Described thinking as directed toward attainment of pleasure and elimination of pain.
4. Galen (A.D. 130–200)	c. Believed that bodily ailments, as well as mental disorders, could result from emotional factors.
	d. Noted the difference between acute and chronic conditions as well as the differences between illusions, hallucinations, and delusions.

    e. What type of treatment did mentally disordered persons usually receive during the years these Greek and Roman physicians and philosophers were influential? (p. 35)

    This treatment ended when the "dark ages of abnormal psychology" began in A.D. _____. (p. 36)

12

f.   The first mental hospital was established in the city of _____
(Turkey) in A.D. _____. The more scientific aspects of Greek and Roman medicine
survived only in Islamic countries.   (p. 36)

2.   Demonology in the middle ages (A.D. 500–1500)
a.   How were the dancing manias, which were considered "abnormal behavior," related to ancient
Greek religious practices?   (p. 37)

b.   Most of the victims persecuted or killed for witchcraft were women, and those who inflicted the
torture were male priests and monks. How have historians interpreted this
observation?   (pp. 41–42)

c.   How were persons who were believed to be witches generally treated?   (p. 42)

d.   Witch-hunts generally ended in Europe in approximately 1500, but in the American colonies they
continued into the _____ century.   (p. 43)

3.   Growth toward humanitarian approaches (A.D. 1500–1900)
a.   The reappearance of humane treatment of disturbed persons can be attributed to four persons.
They were _____, who was the first physician known to speak out
against witchcraft;   (p. 43)
_____, who insisted that dancing mania was a disease and also
advocated treatment by "bodily magnetism," later called hypnosis;   (p. 43)
_____, who was scorned by his peers and whose step-by-step rebuttal
of witchcraft was banned by the church; and finally,   (p. 43)
_____, who wrote that witches were but victims of melancholy, a thesis
that was rejected, banned, and burned by King James I of England.   (p. 44)
b.   Henry VIII of England established a mental hospital in 1545 called St. Mary of Bethlehem,
which soon became known as _____, adding a new word to our
language.   (p. 44)
In 1566 _____, the first hospital in the Americas, was founded. (p. 44)
Describe the atmosphere and treatment methods of these early "hospitals."   (p. 44)

The _____ shrine was one of the few enlightened settings where
humane care of disturbed persons was practiced during this period.   (p. 46)
c.   Humanitarian reform of mental hospitals received its first great impetus from the work of
_____ of France.   (p. 46)

13

Why is his work referred to as an "experiment"? (pp. 46–47)

This great work was begun at _____ hospital and later at
_____ hospital which have become known as the first "modern"
hospitals for the care of the insane. (pp. 46–47)

d. The first trained nurses and supervisors were introduced at the _____
in 1941 by Samuel Hitch. (p. 49)

e. _____ was a famous American physician who wrote the first textbook
on psychiatry in the United States. (p. 49)

The form of treatment he advocated was _____. (p. 49)

This therapy resulted in a discharge rate of _____ percent among patients who had been
ill one year or less and _____ percent among patients who had been ill longer than
one year. (p. 49)

This form of therapy, despite its high degree of success, was abandoned by the late 1800s. Your
text presents five reasons for this loss of influence. What were they? (p. 49)

f. What accomplishments led the United States Congress to pass a resolution in 1901 labeling
_____ as "among the noblest examples of humanity in all
history"? (p. 50)

What type of conditions did this woman find in state institutions at the beginning of her
career? (p. 50)

How did Clifford Beers follow up her work? (pp. 50–51)

4. The foundations of twentieth-century views
a. What was the subject of Clifford Beers' book, *A Mind that Found Itself?* (pp. 50–51)

b. How did the discovery of the cause of general paresis lead to the development of false expectations among researchers? (p. 52)

c. The first clinic to treat behavior disorders from a psychological perspective was founded by
_____ at the University of Pennsylvania in 1896. (p. 52)

(5.) Mental disorders in China
    a. From earliest times, Chinese understanding of mental disorders was based on natural causes, on the concept of yin and yang.   (p. 38)
        Describe how this concept explained the development of mental disorders.   (p. 38)

        How were people with mental disorders treated in China up to A.D. 100?   (p. 38)

    b. What views of mental disorder predominated in China from A.D. 100 to 800?   (p. 38)

CHAPTER QUIZ

1. Which of the following statements regarding the evolution of popular views of psychopathology is *not correct?*
    a. Development has been a steady move forward.
    b. Development began with beliefs based on superstition and ended with beliefs based on scientific awareness.
    c. Many modern scientific concepts have their roots in the past.
    d. The evolution of ideas has been marked with brief periods of advancement followed by long years of destructive backward surges.
2. All of the following techniques are methods to rid the body of demoniacal possession *except*
    a. trephining.
    b. exorcism.
    c. purgatives made of sheep dung.
    d. bleeding.
3. The "father of modern medicine" is
    a. Hippocrates.
    b. Avicenna.
    c. Agrippa.
    d. Phillipe Pinel.
4. Hippocrates erroneously held which of the following beliefs?
    a. The brain is the central organ of human activity.
    b. Head injuries may cause sensory and motor disorders.
    c. Dreams are important in understanding the personality.
    d. There are basically four types of body fluids.
5. Plato and Aristotle anticipated Freud in their emphasis on
    a. humane treatment.
    b. behavior as motivated by "natural appetites" toward the attainment of pleasure and elimination of pain.
    c. the use of insanity as an excuse for crime.
    d. psychological factors, such as frustration and conflict, as causes of disturbed behavior.

6. The physician who kept Greek and Roman medical concepts alive in Islamic countries after the fall of Rome was
   a. Agrippa.
   b. Aristotle.
   c. Asclepiades.
   d. Avicenna.

7. The manual prepared by Sprenger and Kiaemer as a complete guide to the detection and punishment of witches was called the
   a. *Summes Desiderantes Affectibus.*
   b. *Mallus Maleficarum.*
   c. *Deception of Demons.*
   d. *Discovery of Witchcraft.*

8. _____ was an early believer in astral influences.
   a. St. Vincent de Paul
   b. Agrippa
   c. Paracelsus
   d. King James I

9. Advocates of science against demonology included all the following except
   a. Johann Weyer.
   b. Reginald Scot.
   c. King James I.
   d. St. Vincent de Paul.

10. An institution noted for kindness and humanity in the care of the mentally ill was
    a. The Gheel Shrine, Belgium.
    b. La Maison de Charenton, Paris.
    c. St. Mary of Bethlehem, London.
    d. San Hipolito, Mexico.

11. Who unchained the insane?
    a. Phillippe Pinel
    b. Jean Esquirol
    c. William Take
    d. Dorothea Dix

12. What was accomplished by Samuel Hitch?
    a. He unchained the insane.
    b. He founded York retreat.
    c. He began the systematic recording of case histories.
    d. He introduced trained nurses into asylums.

13. The founder of American psychiatry is
    a. William Tuke.
    b. Lightner Witmer.
    c. Benjamin Rush.
    d. Dorothea Dix.

14. All the following are reasons that have been offered as explanations for the abandonment of moral therapy in the latter part of the nineteenth century except:
    a. a rising tide of racial and ethnic prejudice.
    b. overextension of hospital facilities.

c. general loss of faith among the general population.
d. belief that mental disorders would yield to physical solutions.
15. The first person to combine research and application of scientific psychological data was
a. Wilheim Wundt.
b. Wilham Healy.
c. Clifford Beers.
d. Lightner Witmer.

3

Biological, psychosocial, and sociocultural viewpoints

OVERVIEW

The models of abnormal behavior are discussed in this chapter. The biological viewpoint focuses on irregularities in the biochemical functioning of the brain to explain mental disorders. Beginning with the work of two men, Pavlov and Freud, the psychosocial model has grown to include the psychoanalytic, behavioristic, humanistic, and interpersonal viewpoints. Previously, clinicians believed that they had to declare allegiance to one viewpoint or another, but it is now widely recognized that no one model can adequately explain every aspect of every form of abnormal behavior. Consequently, one needs to assess and deal with the interaction of biological, psychosocial, and sociocultural factors to develop the total clinical picture.

TERMS YOU SHOULD KNOW

mesmerism (p. 60)

cathartic method (p. 62)

free association (p. 62)

psychoanalysis (p. 62)

id (p. 62)

libido (p. 62)

pleasure principle (p. 63)

primary process (p. 63)

ego (p. 63)

secondary process (p. 63)

reality principle (p. 63)

superego (p. 63)

intrapsychic conflicts (p. 63)

reality anxiety (p. 63)

neurotic anxiety (p. 63)

moral anxiety (p. 63)

ego defense mechanisms (p. 63)

unconscious (p. 63)

repressed (p. 64)

oral stage (p. 64)

anal stage (p. 64)

phallic stage (p. 64)

latency stage (p. 64)

genital stage (p. 64)

fixated (p. 64)

Oedipus complex (p. 65)

castration anxiety (p. 65)

Electra complex (p. 65)

objects (p. 66)

introjection (p. 66)

separation-individuation (p. 67)

behaviorism (p. 68)

operant (instrumental) conditioning (p. 69)

reinforcement (p. 70)

unconditioned stimulus (p. 70)

unconditioned response (p. 70)

reinforcer (p. 70)

reinforcement (p. 70)

punishment (p. 70)

negative reinforcement (p. 71)

intermittent reinforcement (p. 71)

extinguishes (p. 71)

avoidance conditioning (p. 71)

generalization (p. 71)

discrimination (p. 71)

modeling (p. 72)

shape (p. 72)

primary drives (p. 72)

secondary drives (p. 72)

self-statements (p. 73)

behavior-modification techniques (p. 73)

self-concept (p. 76)

significant others (p. 80)

"good me" (p. 80)

"bad me" (p. 80)

self-system (p. 80)

"not me" (p. 80)

social-exchange view (p. 81)

social roles (p. 81)

games (p. 81)

attribution theory (p. 82)

evaluations (p. 82)

expectations (p. 82)

interpersonal accommodation (p. 82)

cultural relativism (p. 88)

epidemiology (p. 90)

high risk groups (p. 90)

prognosis (p. 90)

interdisciplinary approach (p. 91)

CONCEPTS TO MASTER

1. The biological perspective
   a. The extreme biological viewpoint, held by many medical practitioners states that abnormal behavior is the product of _____ in the brain or elsewhere in the central nervous system. _____ played a role in the early development of the biological viewpoint by developing a system of classification. Why do the authors conclude that the biological viewpoint is inappropriate for the vast majority of abnormal behavior?   (pp. 56–58)

   b. A patient has the delusion that he is Napoleon. How does this delusion reveal that biological causes must interact with experience?   (p. 58)

   c. There is evidence that some mental disorders have a hereditary component. Describe the work on behavioral differences thought to be linked to sex hormone levels.   (p. 59)

   d. How have the development of psychiatric drugs and electric shock therapy (ECT) furthered the credibility of the biological perspective?   (p. 59)

2. The psychoanalytic perspective
   a. Who took the first systematic steps toward understanding psychological factors in mental disorders?   (p. 60)

   b. How is "mesmerism" related to the development of hypnosis?   (pp. 60–61)

   c. Liebeault and Bernheim found that hypnosis "cured" a patient who had had hysteria for some time. What theory about hypnosis and hysteria did they develop as a result?   (p. 61)

   d. What was the impact of the widespread recognition that hysteria was a psychologically caused disorder?   (pp. 61–62)

   e. Freud developed the "cathartic method," using hypnosis differently from the French doctors. How did Freud use hypnosis with his early patients?   (p. 62)

3. Basics of the psychoanalytic perspective
    a. Fill in the empty spaces in the following chart with the correct psychoanalytic concepts.   (pp. 62–63)

Subsystem	Principle of Operation	Type of Thinking	Purpose	Type of Anxiety Generated
id	operates according to _____ principle	engages in mental images and fantasies referred to as _____ thinking	source of two types of instinctual drives: a. _____ b. _____	generates _____ anxiety that results from impulses that, if expressed, would be punished in some way
ego	operates according to _____ principle	uses reason and intellectual resources to deal with external world, which is referred to as _____ _____ thinking	mediates between the _____ and the _____ in such a way as to insure that needs are met and survival assured	generates _____ anxiety that arises from threats in the external world
superego	operates according to _____ principle	mental representation of the taboos and moral values of society	operates through the _____ to inhibit desires that are considered wrong or immoral	generates _____ anxiety which arises from feelings of guilt

b. The ego can cope with anxiety in basically two ways. What are they?   (p. 63)

c. An important psychoanalytic concept is the unconscious. What type of memories, desires, and experiences exist in the unconscious?   (pp. 63–64)

An individual is unaware of unconscious material until it is expressed. How is it expressed?

d. Freud viewed personality development as a succession of stages, each characterized by a dominant mode of achieving sexual pleasure. Fill in the empty spaces on the following chart regarding psychosexual stages. (p. 64)

Stage	Ages	Source of Gratification
oral		
anal	2–3 years	
phallic		self-manipulation of the genitals
latency		
genital		

e. How is the Oedipus complex supposed to be developed? What is considered to be its proper resolution if development proceeds normally? (p. 65)

f. Why is the psychoanalytic viewpoint considered "pessimistic and deterministic"? (p. 66)

g. Modern psychoanalysis emphasizes object-relations theory. Explain. (p. 66)

4. Impact on our views of psychopathology
    a. Freud is credited with developing two techniques for learning about the conscious and unconscious aspects of mental life. What were these? (pp. 67–68)

    b. As a result of applying his techniques to patients, Freud came to emphasize the importance of three factors in determining later personality adjustment or maladjustment. What were these three factors? (pp. 67–68)

c. Is it true that Freud believed abnormal behavior resulted from exaggerated use of normal ego defense mechanisms? (p. 68)

d. Eight major criticisms have been made of the psychoanalytic approach. Following are three of them. Fill in the remaining five. (p. 68)
    1. Psychoanalysts overemphasize the sex drive.
    2. Psychoanalysis is impractical as a treatment.
    3. No scientific evidence exists to support the existence of many of Freud's assumptions or to document the effectiveness of the therapy.
    4.

    5.

    6.

    7.

    8.

5. The behavioristic perspective
    a. Behavioral psychologists believe that the data used by psychoanalysts is unacceptable scientifically. What data do psychoanalysts use? (pp. 68–69)

        What data do behaviorists use instead? (p. 69)

    b. The origins of the behavioristic approach can be traced to the Russian physiologist named _____, but the elaboration of the approach is credited to an American psychologist named _____. (p. 69)
    c. Watson believed that he could take a healthy child and convert it into anything he wanted. Thus, he placed heavy emphasis on the _____ and on the role of _____ in development of personality and behavior. (p. 69)

6. Basic principles of the behavioristic perspective
    a. Place the following statements under the type of learning they describe. (p. 70)
        1. Through conditioning, a response may come to be elicited by a wide range of stimuli.
        2. As we mature, this type of learning becomes more important.
        3. Many responses, particularly those related to fear, are learned through this type of learning.
        4. In this type of learning, the response typically precedes the stimulus.

24

5. As we grow, this type of learning becomes an important mechanism for discriminating the desirable from the undesirable.

Respondent Conditioning   **Operant Conditioning**

1.   1.

2.   2.

                                               3.

b. A learned response is most difficult to extinguish when it has been established by what schedule of reinforcement?   (p. 71)
   Circle the correct answer.
   1. High rate of reinforcement
   2. Intermittent reinforcement

c. Avoidance learning allows an individual to anticipate an adverse event and respond in such a way as to avoid it. How does developing a phobia of dogs (through avoidance learning) lessen anxiety?   (p. 71)

   How resistant to extinction would a dog phobia be without specific treatment?

d. Match the following terms and examples: (pp. 71–72)

   1. discrimination   a. A person, previously bitten, avoids dogs.
   2. generalization   b. An occasional win at gambling keeps the behavior going.
   3. intermittent reinforcement   c. A person, beaten as a child, has a fear of authority.
   4. reinforcement   d. A child performs a response that in the past produced
   5. negative reinforcement   candy.
   6. avoidance conditioning   e. A child performs a response that in the past avoided
   7. shaping   spanking.
                                       f. A child of wealthy parents learns to regard only wealthy
                                          people as worthy.
                                       g. A mute schizophrenic is reinforced for slight lip
                                          movements.

e. List some examples of the following types of drives.   (p. 72)
   Primary drives   Secondary drives

25

f. How has the focus of behaviorism been changed by the "cognitive behavioral" revolution? (p. 73)

7. Impact of behavioristic approach on our views of psychopathology
   a. Behaviorists believe that maladaptive behavior develops in two general ways. What are they? (p. 73)

   b. Complete the following listing of the strengths and criticisms of behaviorism. (p. 73)

Strengths	Criticisms
1. preciseness and objectivity	1. overly concerned with symptoms, ignores values and meaning
2.	2.
3.	

8. The humanistic perspective
   a. What is the focus of the humanistic perspective? (p. 75)

   How is the humanistic perspective at odds with the behavioristic approach?

   How is the humanistic perspective at odds with the psychoanalytic approach?

   b. What are the three "underlying themes and principles" that characterize the humanistic approach? (p. 76)

   c. Following are Carl Rogers' "propositions" about the self-concept. Fill in the missing words. (p. 76)

1. Each individual exists in a private world of which the _____ is the center.
2. The most basic striving of the self is toward maintenance, enhancement, and _____ of the _____.
3. The individual reacts to situations in terms of the way he or she _____ them.
4. Perceived threat to the self is followed by _____.
5. The individual's inner tendencies are toward _____ and wholeness.

9. Impact of the humanistic view on our views of psychopathology
   a. Humanists generally believe that psychopathology is caused by the blocking or distortion of both _____ and _____. (p. 78)
   b. What has been the major impact of the humanistic approach on our thinking about abnormal behavior? (p. 78)

   c. The authors criticize the humanistic approach. What three criticisms do they make? (p. 79)

10. The interpersonal perspective
    a. Theorists who share an interpersonal perspective believe that abnormal behavior is best understood by analyzing a person's _____ both past and present. (p. 79)
    b. The roots of the interpersonal perspective lie in psychoanalysis, but the views have been most fully developed by several theorists who rebelled from the Freudian mold including _____, _____, and _____. (p. 79)
    c. Harry Stack Sullivan believes that development proceeds through various stages, involving different patterns of _____. (p. 80)
    d. Describe how a child comes to label parts of his or her behavior. (pp. 80–81)
       1. "Good me"

       2. "Bad me."

    In time these labels lead to the formulation of the self-system.
    e. Respond to the following questions regarding several other interpersonal theories: (pp. 81–82)
       1. What is a "role expectation"?

2. What are two purposes of "interpersonal games"?

3. Why are the "attributions" we make important?

11. Impact of the interpersonal perspective on our views of psychopathology
    a. On what areas would interpersonal therapy focus?   (p. 83)

    b. What is the major drawback of Sullivan's, as well as later investigators', concepts?   (p. 83)

    c. What has the interpersonal perspective accomplished?   (p. 83)

12. The sociocultural viewpoint
    a. On what causal factors do sociocultural theories of abnormal behavior function?   (p. 84)

    b. How is cross-cultural research a substitute for laboratory studies?   (p. 84)

    c. What are four difficulties in doing cross-cultural research?   (p. 84)

    d. Malinowski found little evidence among the Trobriand Islanders of oedipal conflict. He therefore
       concluded . . .   (p. 84)

       This and other studies led to the formulation of "cultural relativism." Explain this
       doctrine.   (p. 88)

       Is this view widely held today?   (p. 88)

Are the types of serious disorders found in the western world found among all peoples of the world? What features lead behavior to be considered abnormal in any society? (p. 88)

e. There is evidence that culture does influence the particular form mental illness takes. For example, how do Irish and Italians differ in response to illness? Are strong guilt feelings always associated with depression in all parts of the world? (p. 88)

f. Respond to the following questions regarding the research of Faris and Dunham (1939), Jaco (1960), and others:
1. What did these researchers find about the relationship of schizophrenia and place of residence? (p. 88)

2. What information can be learned from "epidemiological" studies such as this one? (p. 90)

3. How can this information be used? (p. 90)

g. What were the three revolutions in mental health? (p. 90)

h. How is the community mental health movement a "revolution"? (p. 90)

13. Toward an interdisciplinary approach
a. It is increasingly apparent that an interaction of biological, psychosocial, and sociocultural factors causes abnormal behavior. A viewpoint which integrates these factors is called the
_____ approach. (p. 91)
b. What has been accomplished on a practical level by this approach? (p. 91)

29

14. Summary chart of ego defense mechanisms
    Place the following ego defense mechanisms in the appropriate blanks: denial of reality, fantasy, repression, rationalization, projection, reaction formation, displacement, intellectualization, undoing, regression, identification, compensation. (pp. 64–65)

Ego Defense Mechanism	**Example**
1. _____	a. A student explains to the teacher why he has neglected studies for cultural pursuits.
2. _____	b. An office worker goes home and is unreasonably angry with her family after being criticized.
3. _____	c. Man scheduled to be executed says, "So they'll kill me, and that's that."
4. _____	d. "Conquering hero" and "suffering hero" are two common patterns.
5. _____	e. Little boy reverts to bedwetting when the new baby comes home.
6. _____	f. Student fails an examination and believes the teacher is to blame.
7. _____	g. College grads are terribly upset if their college doesn't have a winning team.
8. _____	h. Terminally ill persons go through a stage where they refuse to believe they are dying.
9. _____	i. A soldier develops amnesia after seeing a friend killed.
10. _____	j. People become zealous crusaders, often referred to as the "reformed sinner syndrome."
11. _____	k. A child-abusing parent brings home presents.
12. _____	l. Wilma Rudolph, crippled and unable to walk until she is eight years old, becomes an Olympic track winner.

15. Some behavior modification techniques based on learning principles
    a. Match the following three columns. (p. 74)

1. shaping	1. avoidance behavior	1. Physician gave himself a shock when he craved a drug.
2. use of negative reinforcement	2. reinforcement to modify covert behavior	2. Child ate favorite food while a rabbit was in the background.
3. cognitive restructuring	3. reinforcement of successive approximations	3. Subjects learned what to say to themselves during anxiety-arousing situations.
4. desensitization	4. An established behavior pattern is no longer reinforced.	4. Any degree of masculine behavior was rewarded in a feminine boy.

(chart continues on p. 31)

5. withdrawal of reinforcement	5. Conditions that evoke avoidance behavior are paired with positive stimuli.	5. Parents showed children less attention when they they engaged in self-injurious behavior.

16. The existential perspective
    a. What does the existential perspective emphasize?   (p. 77)

    How does this emphasis differ from the humanistic approach?

    b. What is the difference between the existential concepts of "existence" and "essence"? What creates our essence?

    c. What is the "will-to-meaning?"

    d. Explain the significance of death in existential thinking.

(17.) Toward an interpersonal diagnostic system   (p. 80)
    a. Clemore and Benjamin (1979) argue that three serious flaws remain in DSM–III. What are they?
       1.

       2.

       3.

    b. Describe how they suggest the dimensions of autonomy-interdependence, friendliness-hostility, and dominance-submission could be used to build a diagnostic system.

(18.) Unusual patterns of behavior that are considered to be culture bound
    a. Give descriptions and the countries in which each of the following disorders has been observed: (p. 89)

31

1. Windigo

2. Latah

3. Amok

4. Koro

5. Kitsunetsuki.

CHAPTER QUIZ

1. In which of the following diseases does a strict biological causal model appear to be inappropriate?
   a. schizophrenia
   b. toxic psychoses
   c. cerebral arteriosclerosis
   d. senile psychoses
2. A strict biological viewpoint on the cause of abnormal behavior is supported by the observation of
   a. temporary disruptions in brain processes such as those caused by alcohol intoxication.
   b. memory loss.
   c. delusions that vary in content dependent on the client's experience.
   d. biochemical imbalances that may result from stress.
3. Experimental evidence supporting the causal role of biological factors includes
   a. the success of ECT and drug treatments.
   b. tempermental differences in newborns.
   c. sex differences in certain behaviors.
   d. variations in the content of delusions among cultural groups.
4. Important factors in the development of psychoanalysis include all the following *except*
   a. Mesmer's work on animal magnetism.
   b. Berheim and Liebeault's cure of an hysterical client with hypnosis.
   c. Wandt's founding the first psychology laboratory.
   d. Breuer's development of the "cathartic method."
5. Which of the following statements regarding the ego is false?
   a. It operates on the basis of the pleasure principle.
   b. Its logic can be labeled "secondary process" thinking.

c. It mediates between the id and the realities of the external world.

d. It uses reason and other intellectual resources to accomplish its goals.

6. Which type of anxiety is a signal to the ego that an unacceptable impulse is threatening to break out?

   a. reality anxiety
   b. neurotic anxiety
   c. moral anxiety
   d. free-floating anxiety

7. Object-relation theorists, in contrast to strict adherents of psychoanalysis, place emphasis on

   a. values and meaning.
   b. Electra complex.
   c. symbolic representations of significant others.
   d. ego defense mechanisms.

8. Psychoanalytic views that have made enduring contributions to understanding abnormal behavior include all the following *except:*

   a. Abnormal behavior is an attempt to cope with difficult problems.
   b. Motives toward personal growth are an important force in personality development.
   c. The techniques of free association and dream analysis can be used to explore the unconscious.
   d. Abnormal behavior results from overuse of defensive mechanisms.

9. The form of learning where an individual learns to achieve a desired goal is

   a. respondent conditioning.
   b. operant conditioning.
   c. modeling.
   d. avoidance conditioning.

10. Rewarding a behavior that is in the right direction even though it does not reflect the final form is

    a. intermittent reinforcement.
    b. generalization.
    c. discrimination.
    d. shaping.

11. The behavioristic tradition has been criticized for

    a. its precision and objectivity.
    b. its research orientation.
    c. failure to demonstrate effectiveness.
    d. overconcern with symptoms.

12. Which of the following statements regarding the humanistic perspective is *false?*

    a. It focuses on conscious experiences.
    b. It differs from behaviorism in its greater emphasis on inner experience.
    c. It differs from psychoanalysis in its more optimistic view of human beings.
    d. It emphasizes prior causes to uncover the complexities of behavior.

13. According to the humanistic view, psychopathology is caused by all the following except

    a. conflict between biological drives (primarily sexual) and reality factors.
    b. exaggerated use of ego defense mechanisms.
    c. unfavorable social conditions and faulty learning.
    d. excessive stress.

14. An anthropologist has located a society where sisters marry their brothers. According to the doctrine of cultural relativism, this evidence suggests that brother-sister incest

    a. is a mental disorder.

b. cannot be a mental disorder.

c. may be a mental disorder, there are no universal standards.

d. should be subject to the anthropologist veto and viewed as a mental disorder.

15. Epidemiological studies have revealed that the incidence of

a. psychosis is three times higher in rural than urban areas.

b. psychosis is higher among married people than among divorced and separated people.

c. schizophrenia is higher among higher socioeconomic groups.

d. hospital admissions decrease with greater distance from inner city areas.

4

Causal factors in abnormal behavior

OVERVIEW

The potentials for maladaptive outcome within the normal developmental process are discussed in depth in this chapter. A large number of research studies are introduced in the chapter to illustrate the current state of knowledge regarding biological, psychosocial, or sociocultural factors that may, directly or indirectly, cause various types of abnormal behavior. The chapter can seem overwhelming at first, because so many potential causal factors are discussed. Luckily, not all are applicable to any given client that one deals with clinically.

TERMS YOU SHOULD KNOW

etiology (p. 94)

primary cause (p. 94)

predisposing cause (p. 94)

precipitating cause (p. 94)

reinforcing cause (p. 94)

causal pattern (p. 95)

self-regulating system (p. 95)

diathesis (p. 96)

stress (p. 96)

chromosomal anomalies (p. 97)

faulty genes (p. 98)

35

autosomes (p. 98)

sex chromosomes (p. 98)

X chromosomes (p. 98)

Y chromosomes (p. 98)

Down's syndrome (p. 98)

trisomy (p. 98)

Klinefelter's syndrome (pp. 98–100)

genes (p. 101)

DNA (p. 101)

dominant gene (p. 101)

recessive gene (p. 101)

polygenetic (p. 101)

proband or index case (p. 102)

monozygotic twins (p. 102)

concordance rates (p. 102)

constitutional (p. 102)

physique (p. 102)

cogenital defect (p. 103)

primary reaction tendencies (p. 104)

neurotransmitter (p. 106)

homeostasis (p. 106)

hospitalism syndrome (p. 108)

self (p. 109)

cognitive map (p. 109)

self-identity (p. 109)

assimilated (p. 110)

accommodation (p. 110)

self-ideal (p. 110)

life-style (p. 110)

inner controls (p. 110)

socialized (p. 110)

critical periods (p. 111)

cognitive dissonance (p. 113)

motivation (p. 116)

selective vigilance (p. 116)

perceptual defense (p. 116)

hierarchy of needs (p. 117)

deficiency motivation (p. 117)

growth motivation (p. 117)

motive pattern (p. 117)

level of aspiration (p. 117)

parental deprivation (p. 119)

affectionless psychopathy (p. 120)

failure to thrive (p. 120)

difficult baby (p. 123)

dissonant stress (p. 105)

autistic (p. 123)

negative model (p. 128)

discordant family (p. 129)

disturbed family (p. 129)

marital schism (p. 129)

marital skew (p. 129)

disrupted family (p. 129)

inadequate family (p. 131)

antisocial family (p. 131)

social roles (p. 133)

androgyny (p. 133)

differential participation (p. 133)

disorder-engendering social role (p. 134)

future shock (p. 136)

CONCEPTS TO MASTER

1. Perspectives on causation
   a. Fill in the causal factors, emphasized by each of the following models of psychopathology. (p. 93)

Viewpoint	Factors Leading to Psychopathology
biological viewpoint	
psychoanalytic viewpoint	
behavioristic viewpoint	
humanistic/existential viewpoint	
interpersonal viewpoint	
sociocultural viewpoint	

   b. Label the following diagrams with the appropriate term from the following: causal factor, causal pattern, feedback loop.
      1. A + B + C ────────────► condition Y   (pp. 95–96)

      2.

      A

      B

      Condition Y

      3. X ────────────────────►condition Y
   c. Explain what the authors mean by a "diathesis-stress" model of abnormal behavior.   (p. 96)

2. Genetic endowment as a determinant
   a. A fertilized human egg contains 46 chromosomes arranged in 23 pairs. Twenty-two pairs, called
      _____, determine general anatomical and physiological characteristics.
      The remaining pair is called _____ chromosomes and determines the
      individual's sex.   (p. 98)
   b. What two conditions, mentioned in the text, result from
      1. an extra autosome (#21)   (p. 98)

      2. an extra X chromosome in a male child?   (pp. 98–99)

   c. What is the estimated incidence of gross chromosomal abnormalities in newborn babies?   (p. 100)

   d. Have chromosomal irregularities been found in schizophrenics?   (p. 100)

   e. Why are females less vulnerable to genetic defects?   (p. 100)

   f. Place the words *chromosome* and *gene* in the proper location on the following diagram.   (p. 98)

   1. _____   2. _____

   g. What do the authors mean when they say that genes can affect behavior only
       "indirectly"?   (p. 101)

   h. Are the genetic influences on abnormal behavior thought to mainly involve dominant and
       recessive genes?   (p. 101)

If not, what form of genetic influence is believed to be most relevant? (p. 101)

    i.   Most of the information we have concerning the role of faulty genes is obtained through the family history method. Explain how this method works. (pp. 101–102)

    j.   Will a person who inherits a genetic endowment for schizophrenia inevitably develop that disease? (p. 102)

Which is the *most likely* outcome in a genetically affected person, occurrence or nonoccurrence of the disorder? (p. 102)

3. Constitutional liabilities
    a.   Two constitutional factors are bodily physique and physical attractiveness. Have these two factors been found to affect the way an individual acts? (p. 102)

The way others treat the individual? (p. 102)

The feelings an individual has about himself or herself? (pp. 102–103)

    b.   Respond to the following questions regarding the research of Snyder, Tanke, and Berscheid (1977). (pp. 102–103)
        1.   What did these researchers do?

        2.   What results did they obtain?

        3.   What does this study suggest about the impact of constitutional factors?

    c.   How many babies are born with mental or physical handicaps per 100 live births? (p. 103)

What is the most frequent general class of causes for these handicaps? (p. 103)

d. Low birth weight (prematurity) is the most common birth difficulty associated with later mental disorders. What are the major factors known to place a fetus at high risk for prematurity? (p. 103)

e. An infant's sensitivity to stimuli, temperament, and activity level are examples of primary reaction tendencies. Respond to these questions related to this concept.
   1. Recent research has indicated that certain differences between men and women are caused by early hormonal influences. Pervin concluded that these differences involved what behaviors? (p. 104)

   2. What is a "difficult baby?" (pp. 104–105)

   3. What happens if there is a poor fit between environment and a child's temperament? (p. 105)

4. Brain dysfunction
   a. How frequently does brain dysfunction contribute to vulnerability to mental disorder? (p. 105)

   b. How many older persons have mental disorders attributable to brain dysfunction? (p. 105)

5. Physical deprivation
   a. Describe what happens when subjects are deprived of sleep for 72–98 hours. (p. 106)

   b. Refer to the study by Keys (1950).
      1. What was done? (pp. 106–107)

      2. What were the results? (p. 107)

c. How does malnutrition during the first year of life affect the physical development of the brain? (p. 107)

Are these effects permanent? (p. 107)

What are the estimates of the extent of childhood malnutrition in the world? (p. 107)

6. Self as a determinant
   a. Human infants begin life with a high degree of modifiability and capacity to learn from experience. What price do we pay for this flexibility? (p. 109)

   b. Our "cognitive map" is the rules or assumptions that govern how we see the world. New information may be distorted in order to fit the rules. This process is called
   _____. Alternately, in a process called
   _____ the rules may be changed as a result of the new information. (pp. 109–110)

   c. Piaget and others have shown that human development procedes in a sequence. What happens if developmental tasks are not mastered at the appropriate stage? (p. 111)

   d. What are the three possible outcomes the authors mention if needed stimulation and learning are lacking during early critical periods? (p. 112)

   e. Mischel (1973) has observed that several learning-based differences become apparent very early in the development of young children. Describe how children may differ in: (p. 112)
      1. competence

      2. processing of information

      3. expectations

      4. experiences they seek

5. coping with impulses

How long are these differences expected to be important?

f. The following chart summarizes the basic core of psychological strivings that are the psychological requirements for healthy development. Briefly describe each striving. (pp. 112–116)

Psychological Striving	Description	Example
1. understanding, order, predictability (pp. 112–113)		attempts by primitive people to describe the origin of fire
2. adequacy, competence, security (p. 113)		preference for jobs with security
3. love, belonging, approval (pp. 113–114)		need for human contact as death approaches
4. self-esteem, worth, identity (p. 114)		undergoing sex change operations
5. values, meaning, hope (pp. 114–115)		prisoners of war who lost hope and died
6. personal growth and fulfillment (pp. 115–116)		wondering "Who am I?"

7. Motivation and behavior
  a. Activation can vary from very low to very high. List several factors that can affect one's level of activation. (p. 116)
    1.

    2.

    3.

The following figure illustrates the effect of emotional activation on problem solving and task performance. According to the figure, when is task performance most efficient?   (p. 116)

When is it least efficient?

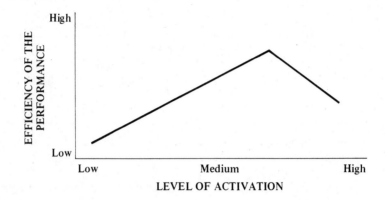

b.   The tendency of people to screen out or distort information that is incompatible with their expectations demonstrates the impact of motivation on which psychological process?   (p. 116)

Two other psychological processes are affected by the motives active in an individual. What are they?   (p. 117)

c.   The following figure illustrates what Maslow has named the _____ of needs.   (p. 117)

44

d. Some people are primarily concerned with love and relations with others with material possessions and power. These essential elements of an individual's life-style are referred to as his/her _____. When goals are far beyond an individual's capacity, we speak of an unrealistically high _____.
Are motive patterns constant over time? (p. 117)

8. Early deprivation and trauma
   a. Describe the consequences of parental deprivation from each of the following theoretical viewpoints. (p. 119)
      1. Freud (psychoanalysis): The consequences of parental deprivation are . . .

      2. Skinner (behaviorism): The consequences of parental deprivation are . . .

      3. Rogers (humanism): The consequences of parental deprivation are . . .

      4. Sullivan (interpersonal psychology): The consequences of parental deprivation are . . .

9. Parental deprivation
   a. Respond to the following questions regarding the research of Provence and Lipton (1962).
      1. Which two groups of infants were compared in this study? (p. 119)

      2. How did the two groups differ at one year of age? (p. 119)

      3. What have other studies (such as Beres and Obers, 1950) found about the long-range effects of early parental deprivation? (p. 120)

b. What is a common syndrome found by Beres and Obers (1950) among children who were institutionalized before the age of one year?   (p. 120)

c. Burnstein (1981) concluded that abandoned children were characterized by excessive levels of _____, _____, and _____.   (p. 120)

d. To what extent can early deprivation be made up for by abundant love at a later time?   (p. 120)

e. Are "polymatic" children and children placed in day care at an early age as well adjusted as "monomatic" children?   (p. 120)

f. Which of the following groups of children represent the largest number of cases of severe parental deprivation?   (p. 120)
   1. Children separated from parents

   2. Children cared for at home by their parents.

g. Describe the characteristics of adults who were abused as children according to: (p. 121)
   1. Pringle (1965)

   2. Yates (1981).

h. Why do parents reject and abuse their children?   (p. 121)

i. What are the three reasons the authors give to explain the observation that psychic traumas in infancy or early childhood are especially damaging?   (p. 122)

Do traumatic events in childhood always have negative consequences?   (p. 122)

10. Inadequate parenting
   a. How is the child's own temperament and personality an important determinant of the quality of the parent-child relationship? (p. 121)

   b. Fill in the missing data in the following summary chart of faulty parent-child relationships.

Undesirable Condition	Typical Effect on Child's Personality Development
1. rejection (p. 121)	
3.	submissiveness, lack of self-reliance, dependence, low self-evaluation, some dulling of intellectual striving (p. 123)
2. unrealistic moral standards (p. 124)	
4. overpermissiveness/overindulgence (pp. 124–125)	
5. lack of discipline (p. 126)	
6.	fear, hatred of parent, little initiative or spontaneity, lack of friendly feelings toward others (p. 126)
7. inconsistent discipline (p. 126)	
8.	tendency toward confusion, lack of integrated frame of reference, unclear self-identity, lack of initiative, self-devaluation (p. 130)
9. undesirable parental models (p. 128)	

What kind of personal behaviors demonstrate "overprotectiveness"? (pp. 123–124)

What is the usual reason that mothers or fathers would overprotect a child? (p. 123)

d. How does an overly indulged child act? (p. 125)

e. How is a child subjected to overly severe punishment as well as high moral standards likely to grow up? (p. 126)

What happens if the parents are severely restrictive as well? (p. 126)

How does the child subjected to *physical,* as opposed to verbal, discipline often turn out? (p. 126)

f. When is a parent considered an "undesirable parental model"? (p. 128)

Do children always (or often) grow up to show the undesirable behavior of their parents, according to studies such as Kadushin (1967)? (p. 128)

11. Pathogenic family structures
    a. Describe the following types of families:
       1. the discordant family (p. 129)

       2. the disturbed family (p. 129)

3. the disrupted family (p. 129)

4. the inadequate family (p. 131)

5. the antisocial family. (p. 131)

b. It is estimated that at any one time over _____ percent of the population that has ever been married is divorced or separated according to Bloom, Asher, and White (1978). (p. 129)

c. What have Bloom et al. (1978) concluded about the impact of family disruption on development of mental disorders? (p. 130)

d. How can absence of a father affect the development of girls? (pp. 130–131)

e. How can the long-range effects of family disruption on children be minimized? (p. 131)

f. Fill in the missing information on the following diagram, which illustrates recent thinking about the role of disrupted families in the development of juvenile delinquency. (p. 131)

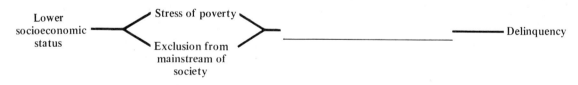

12. Sociocultural environment as a determinant
    a. Certain social roles people can adopt such as excessive femininity has been linked with . . . (p. 133)

b. Explain the following statement: An inverse correlation exists between social class and the prevalence of abnormal behavior. (p. 133)

There are two explanations for the above relationship. Explain each.
1. social drift (p. 133)

2. social stress (p. 134)

c. How did Zimbardo (1975) demonstrate that the role of prison guard is a "disorder engendering social role"? (p. 134)

d. What happens to the rates of mental illness, suicide, and crime during hard economic times? (p. 135)

13. Season of birth—the most puzzling vulnerability factor
In what months are the birth dates of schizophrenics disproportionately concentrated? (p. 95)

14. Predisposing causes of depressive reactions to rape (p. 97)
Describe the relationship of post-rape symptomatology to
1. level of trauma during rape

2. post-rape level of support

3. level of prior functioning.

15. Separation from parents as a traumatic experience

    a. Describe the stages children two through five years of age go through when separated from their parents.

    b. At what age is a child most vulnerable to long-term separation or loss?

CHAPTER QUIZ

1. The expression "the straw that broke the camel's back" could refer to the _____ cause of abnormal behavior.
   a. primary
   b. predisposing
   c. precipitating
   d. reinforcing
2. In abnormal psychology there are few disorders attributed to
   a. single causal factors.
   b. causal patterns.
   c. self-regulating systems.
   d. feedback loops.
3. An example of a disorder caused by autosomal abnormalities is
   a. Huntington's chorea.
   b. Down's syndrome.
   c. Klinefelter's syndrome.
   d. Turner's syndrome.
4. Most forms of mental disorder that are due mainly to faulty genes can be explained in terms of
   a. dominant genes.
   b. recessive genes.
   c. sex chromosomes.
   d. polygenetic inheritance.
5. Which of the following is an example of a primary reaction tendency?
   a. emotional disturbance
   b. sensitivity to stimuli
   c. low birth weight
   d. mental retardation
6. Which of the following statements is false?
   a. Organic brain pathology is a major source of vulnerability to mental disorders in 50 percent of younger populations.
   b. Seventeen percent of persons over 65 have significant brain damage.
   c. Five percent of persons over 60 develop psychiatric symptoms.
   d. The elderly occupy 20 percent of the beds in mental hospitals.
7. Keys (1950) studied volunteers subjected to semistarvation and reported all the following *except:*
   a. subjects become irritable and unsociable.

b. subjects resorted to stealing and lying to get additional food.

c. subjects experienced a marked reduction in sexual interest.

d. subjects' predominant mood was euphoria.

8. All the following are true statements regarding failure to maintain homeostasis except:

a. prolonged disruption of homeostasis can threaten survival.

b. we must sleep to stay sane.

c. few institutionalized infants die from lack of stimulation.

d. severe malnutrition results in irreversible brain damage in infants.

9. Changing your opinion as a result of a political speech is an example of

a. flexible cognitive style.

b. accommodation.

c. assimilation.

d. cognitive dissonance.

10. A child is neglected and rejected in the first year of life during the "critical period" for the formation of basic trust. Which of the following outcomes is least likely to occur?

a. Basic trust may never appear.

b. Basic trust may be slower to develop.

c. Basic trust will develop only partially.

d. Basic trust will develop normally if extra attention is given during the second year.

11. A wealthy businessperson drives from the suburbs to downtown everyday without ever noticing the inner city poverty and deprivation along the way. This could reflect

a. perceptual defense.

b. selective vigilance.

c. cognitive dissonance.

d. deficiency motivation.

12. Follow-up studies of children institutionalized at an early age, particularly before one year of age, have revealed that they demonstrate high frequencies of all the following *except:*

a. affectionless psychopathy.

b. excessive aggressiveness.

c. psychotic behavior.

d. antiweak, antitrust orientations to the world.

13. Childhood trauma is thought to be especially damaging for all the following reasons except:

a. childhood learning occurs in the context of strong emotions.

b. childhood learning generalizes.

c. childhood traumas are more serious than the trauma that affects adults.

d. childhood learning is emotional, not cognitive.

14. Spoiled, selfish, and inconsiderate children are most likely to have had a background of parental

a. inconsistency.

b. unrealistic moral standards.

c. overprotectiveness.

d. overindulgence.

15. A family in which one or both parents is not gaining satisfaction is called a (an) _____ family.

a. discordant

b. disrupted

c. disturbed

d. inadequate

5

Stress and adjustment disorders

OVERVIEW

The chapter begins with a detailed discussion of stress, a topic of critical importance to this "age of anxiety." An understanding of the potential sources of stress, the functional equivalence of biological, psychological, and sociocultural sources of stress, and the general strategies for coping with stressful demands is probably the single most relevant topic to the average person that is presented in this text.

The reactions of individuals to war, concentration camps, and civilian disasters are described and can be viewed as case studies of human functioning under levels of severe stress. The chapter described the coping techniques used by individuals in these situations and the symptoms that appear as the coping techniques fail to eliminate the stress. It will seem unbelievable when reading about some of the situations that there were *any* people who could cope without developing severely abnormal behavior. The practical implications of this chapter will help us improve the way we can prepare people who will face stressful situations, such as surgery, to cope more effectively.

TERMS YOU SHOULD KNOW

stress (p. 142)

stressor (p. 142)

eustress (p. 142)

distress (p. 142)

frustration (p. 142)

conflict (p. 142)

approach-avoidance conflicts (p. 143)

double-approach conflicts (p. 143)

double-avoidance conflicts (p. 144)

pressures (p. 144)

chronic (p. 147)

acute (p. 147)

crisis (p. 147)

holistic (p. 148)

adrenaline (p. 149)

cultural lag (p. 150)

task-oriented (p. 150)

defense-oriented (pp. 150–151)

denial of reality (p. 151)

repression (p. 152)

emotional insulation (p. 152)

intellectualization (isolation) (p. 152)

regression (p. 152)

decompensation (p. 153)

general adaptation syndrome (p. 154)

adjustment disorder (p. 156)

post-traumatic stress disorder (p. 157)

disaster syndrome (p. 163)

panic (p. 167)

startle reactions (p. 170)

proximity (p. 176)

expectancy (p. 176)

immediacy (p. 176)

DDD (p. 180)

CONCEPTS TO MASTER

1. Categories of stressors
   a. Adjustive demands, also known as _____, stem from a variety of sources including biological, psychological, and sociocultural conditions. Give an example of: (p. 142)
      1. a biological stressor

      2.   a psychological stressor

      3.   a sociocultural stressor

  b. When does frustration occur? (p. 142)

  c. When does conflict cause stress? (p. 142)

  d. When does pressure lead to stress? (p. 144)

  e. Match the following terms with the examples that correctly illustrate them:

Term		Example
1. frustration	(p. 142)	a. A mixed blessing dilemma in which some positive and negative features must be accepted, no matter what the decision.
2. approach-avoidance conflict	(p. 143)	
3. double-avoidance conflict	(p. 144)	
4. double-approach conflict	(p. 143)	b. A plus-plus conflict, choosing between two desirable alternatives.
5. pressure	(p. 144)	c. Finals week with a part-time job, studying, and social obligations.
		d. Finding out that the women's basketball team must travel four to a room, but the men's team has only two per room.
		e. A minus-minus conflict, choosing between two undesirable alternatives.

2. Factors influencing the severity of stress
  a. How is the severity of stress gauged or measured? (p. 145)

  b. On what factors does the actual degree of disruption depend? (p. 145)
      1. On the biological level

      2. On the psychological level

  c. Indicate how each of the following have been found to influence the degree of disruption that occurs as a result of stress:

1. the importance of the stressor (p. 145)

2. the length of time the stressor operates (p. 145)

3. the number of stressors operative at any time (p. 145)

4. the opportunity to anticipate the stressor (p. 145)

5. the individual's perception of his or her ability to handle the stress (p. 146)

6. stress tolerance of the individual (p. 146)

7. the personal and material supports available to the individual (p. 146)

3. Stressor patterns are unique and changing
   a. Why are "crises" especially stressful? (p. 147)

   b. The authors estimate that a crisis occurs in the life of the average person once
      every _____. (p. 148)
   c. How can the outcome of a crisis affect a person's subsequent adjustment? (p. 148)

4. General principles of reactions to stress
   a. Place the following levels of coping in the appropriate square: (p. 148)
      1. learned coping patterns
      2. immunological defenses against disease
      3. religious organizations
      4. self-defenses
      5. damage-repair mechanisms
      6. labor unions

Levels of Coping	Examples
1. biological level	
2. psychological-interpersonal level	
3. sociocultural level	

    b.   What does it mean to say that the body's reactions to stress are "holistic"?   (p. 148)

    c.   In the example of the driver having a traffic accident, which bodily processes were inhibited, and which were excited?   (p. 149)

    d.   What does it mean to say that the body's reaction to stress is "economical"?   (p. 149)

    e.   How are the body's reactions to stress "automatic"?   (p. 150)

    f.   How do reactions to stress affect the emotions?   (p. 150)

5. Defense-oriented reaction patterns
    a.   Two types of defense mechanisms are described in the text. What are they?   (p. 151)

    b.   In what three ways do defense mechanisms protect the individual from internal and external threats?   (p. 151)
        1.

2.

3.

c. Place the following ego defense mechanisms in the appropriate blanks: denial of reality, repression, emotional insulation, intellectualization, regression. (pp. 151–153)

Ego defense mechanism	Example
	An American hostage in Iran thinks, "This isn't happening to me."
	After a young woman dies people tell her husband, "Well, she lived a full life."
	An unemployed person becomes apathetic and resigned
	A child who has just gotten a new brother says, "Feed me like a baby, Mom."
	A soldier cannot remember any details of the battle in which his friend was killed.

d. In what ways are defense mechanisms adaptive? (p. 153)

How are they maladaptive? (p. 153)

6. Decompensation under excessive stress
   a. Describe how severe stress (pp. 153–154)
      1. lowers adaptive efficiency

      2. lowers resistance to other stressors

3. causes wear and tear on the organism

b. Personality decompensation under extreme stress appears to follow a course resembling biological decompensation, which consists of three stages: alarm and mobilization, resistance, exhaustion and disintegration.
Describe the behavior of the individual during each stage. (pp. 154–156)

Stage	Behavior of Organism
alarm and mobilization (p. 155)	
stage of resistance (p. 155)	
stage of exhaustion (pp. 155–156)	

7. Adjustment disorders: reactions to difficult life stressors
   a. There are several subclasses of adjustment disorder that are defined by the predominant symptom. Give examples of the subclasses. (p. 156)

   b. In an adjustment disorder the stressor is _____ whereas in post-traumatic stress disorder the stressor is _____. (p. 156)
   c. Describe the three major symptoms of a post-traumatic stress disorder. (p. 157)

   d. Explain the difference between acute post-traumatic stress disorder, chronic post-traumatic stress disorder, and delayed post-traumatic stress disorder. (p. 157)

   e. 1. The first reaction to death of a loved one is _____. Then feelings of _____ overwhelm the person, sometimes punctuated by brief periods of _____. This phase ends by the time of the funeral. (p. 159)

2. The next two or three weeks are characterized by _____. (p. 159)
3. The mourner's acute symptoms subside after how long? (p. 159)

8. Reactions to catastrophic events
   a. Persons who face a civilian disaster commonly show behavior that has been divided into three stages. Fill in the box with the behavior that is typical of each stage. (p. 163)

Stage	Behavior Observed (p. 163)
shock stage	
suggestible stage	
recovery stage	

   b. In which stage does acute post-traumatic stress disorder develop? (p. 163)

   c. The symptoms of post-traumatic stress syndrome (both chronic and delayed) are: (pp. 165–166)
      1. *anxiety,* commonly associated with
         _____ (pp. 165–166)
      2. *tension* often accompanied by _____ (p. 166)
      3. *repetitive nightmares* which serve to
         _____ (p. 166)
      4. *impaired concentration and memory*
      5. *depression.*
   d. Explain why the symptoms caused by stress during each stage of reaction occur.
      1. Shock stage symptoms: stunned, dazed, numbed. These symptoms stem from
         _____. (p. 166)
      2. Stage of suggestibility symptoms stem from
         _____. (p. 167)
      3. Stage of recovery symptoms: recurrent nightmares and need to talk about the disaster. These symptoms appear to be mechanisms for
         _____. (p. 167)
      4. The anxiety that often accompanies these symptoms appears to stem from the realization that _____. (p. 167)
   e. What type of treatment is usually sufficient to lead to rapid alleviation of the symptoms of post-traumatic stress? (p. 167)

There is disagreement over the percentage of disaster victims who require treatment. Kingston and Rosser (1974) estimated that _____ percent required treatment. Parker (1974) found that _____ percent of the victims showed symptoms of disorder.   (p. 168)

9. Traumatic reactions to military combat
    a. According to the government figures presented in your text, what has been the trend in the incidence of combat exhaustion from World War II to the Vietnam War?   (pp. 169–170)

    What are the reasons given to account for this trend?   (p. 170)

    b. What percentage of men can be expected to develop combat exhaustion?   (pp. 169–170)
    c. How does the clinical picture of combat exhaustion differ between combat troops and air corps personnel?   (p. 171)

    d. What are usually the first symptoms of combat exhaustion?   (p. 171)

    e. When combat exhaustion cases reach the aid station, do they differ from each other in the type of symptoms each presents, or do they differ only in the severity of symptoms?   (p. 171)

    f. Under what circumstances might a soldier become amnesic for an entire battle?   (p. 171)

    g. In the Vietnam war, as opposed to World War II, soldiers were seldom exposed to prolonged periods of shelling and bombardment. What effect did this difference have on the combat reactions that were seen in Vietnam?   (p. 172)

    h. What is the "common core" in all cases of combat exhaustion, regardless of the war?   (p. 172)

    i. Why do wounded soldiers show less anxiety than other soldiers?   (p. 172)

    j. Do constitutional differences in vigor, temperament, and sensitivity affect a soldier's resistance to combat exhaustion?   (p. 172)

k. What function do recurrent nightmares play in combat exhaustion cases?   (p. 173)

l. What did Merbaum and Hefez (1976) find about the role of previous psychological adjustment in determining a soldier's vulnerability to combat exhaustion?   (p. 174)

m. What would be the purpose of teaching military officers to foster group identification among soldiers?   (p. 175)

n. What lessons about the most effective procedures for treating combat exhaustion were learned in World War II?   (p. 176)

o. What were the six most common feelings Shatan (1978) found in his study of veterans being treated for post-traumatic stress?   (p. 177)
    1.

    2.

    3.

    4.

    5.

    6.

p. What has been found by Strange and Brown (1970) regarding the residual effects among combat and noncombat veterans?   (p. 178)

q. How did Worthington (1978) characterize the premilitary adjustment of soldiers who experienced difficulty adjusting to the Vietnam war?   (p. 178)

10. Reactions of prisoners of war and concentration camp survivors
    a. What is the DDD syndrome?   (pp. 180–181)

What kinds of activities on the part of the captors can lead to the development of the DDD syndrome in POWs?

b. Usano et al. (1981) conducted an evaluation of 325 air force officers who had been prisoners of war in North Vietnam. Describe their findings regarding   (p. 181)
   1. frequency of psychiatric diagnoses

   2. effect of length of imprisonment.

c. What is the "re-entry" problem?   (p. 182)

d. Describe the residual damage found among survivors of Nazi concentration camps.   (p. 182)

e. Why is it problematic to conclude that survivors of concentration camps carry serious psychological scars as several studies (e.g., Krystal, 1968) have suggested?   (p. 183)

11. Prevention of stress disorders: emotional "inoculation"
   a. Janis (1958) studied students before and after surgery. What did he learn about the relationship of preoperative fear and postoperative adjustment?   (p. 184)

   How does Janis explain the importance of the "work of worrying" to postoperative adjustment?   (p. 184)

   b. Meichenbaum (1973, 1975) and his colleagues have developed a cognitive-behavioral approach which is called "stress-inoculation training" to preparing individuals for stressful events. Describe the methods employed during each of the stages of the procedure on the chart on p. 64.   (pp. 184–185)

Stage	Techniques
first	
second	
third	

(12.) Measuring life stress   (p. 149)
    a. What is an "LCU"?

    b. What happens if a person accumulates more than 300 LCUs in one year?

(13.) Afteraffects of rape
    a. Discuss how each of the following variables are thought to affect a woman's response to
       rape: (p. 164)
       1. relationship to the offender

       2. age

       3. marital status

    b. Describe the coping behavior of the rape victim during the following phases of response to
       rape.   (pp. 164–165)
       1. anticipatory phase

       2. impact phase

       3. post-traumatic recoil phase

4. reconstitution phase

c. What features of the victim determine the severity of post-rape after affects? (p. 165)

(14.) Residual effects of combat exhaustion among outpatients at a VA clinic
Describe the residual symptoms among combat veterans who experienced combat exhaustion compared to combat veterans who did not experience combat exhaustion. (p. 177)

(15.) Failure to readjust after captivity: a tragic ending
   a. Selkin and Loya (1979) conducted a "psychological autopsy." What kind of information is needed for this type of inquiry? (p. 182)

   b. What were the psychologists' conclusions regarding the cause of Jerry L's suicide? (p. 182)

   c. How were their conclusions similar to the reasons the police officer in San Diego sought counseling during the air crash clean-up? (p. 169)

CHAPTER QUIZ

1. Working at a job that was unfulfilling would probably lead to feelings of
   a. conflict.
   b. frustration.
   c. pressure.
   d. defensiveness.
2. A person wants to accept a party invitation because he is very social but is concerned because there will be a lot of drinking and he is a member of AA (Alcoholics Anonymous). He is experiencing a/an
   a. mixed blessing dilemma.
   b. approach-avoidance conflict.
   c. double-avoidance conflict.
   d. double-approach conflict.
3. All the following influence the severity of stress affecting a person *except*
   a. individual stress tolerance.
   b. other stressors operating at the time.

  c. absolute threat value of the stressor.

  d. external resources and supports.

4. When the stress situation approaches or exceeds an individual's adaptive capacity, the situation is referred to as a/an

  a. chronic stress.

  b. acute stress.

  c. eustress.

  d. crisis.

5. Stress reactions have all the following characteristics *except*

  a. they are automatic.

  b. they entail emotions.

  c. they are atomistic.

  d. they are economical.

6. An unhappily married woman is asked at the maternity ward to give her name. She is unable momentarily to remember her married name but can give her maiden name. Her behavior might reveal the defense mechanism of

  a. denial of reality.

  b. repression.

  c. regression.

  d. emotional insulation.

7. Defense mechanisms have all the following characteristics *except*

  a. they are learned.

  b. they are automatic.

  c. they involve self-deception and reality distortion.

  d. they serve useful protective functions and rarely interfere with effective resolution of problems.

8. Which of the following statements is not supported by psychological research?

  a. Stress may influence the growth of cancer.

  b. After a very successful experience, rest can completely restore an individual.

  c. Acute stage fright may disrupt performance.

  d. Soldiers in combat may have a lowered resistance to infection.

9. The alarm and mobilization stage of personality decompensation under excessive stress is characterized by

  a. emotional arousal, increased tension, alertness.

  b. exaggerated and inappropriate defensive measures.

  c. lowering of integration.

  d. rigidity as the individual clings to accustomed defenses.

10. In _____ disorder the stressor is uncommon and the disorder begins immediately or soon after the trauma.

  a. adjustment disorder

  b. acute post-traumatic stress disorder

  c. chronic post-traumatic stress disorder

  d. delayed post-traumatic stress disorder

11. During bereavement, semidazed behavior punctuated by attacks of irritability and anger are *most typical*

  a. for several days immediately after the loss.

  b. for 2–3 weeks after the funeral.

c. for 1–2 months after returning to work.

d. up to one year after the loss.

12. The stages of reaction to a tornado or other disaster are

a. anticipatory, impact, post-traumatic record, and recovery stages.

b. shock, anger, and acceptance stages.

c. shock, suggestible, and recovery stages.

d. alarm and mobilization, resistance, and exhaustion stages.

13. Panic occurs when

a. the group is in the immediate area of a disaster.

b. there is a prearranged plan for dealing with the disaster.

c. a warning of the impending disaster has been sounded.

d. when escape is possible for only a short time.

14. Combat exhaustion was responsible for 1.5 percent of medical discharges during

a. World War I.

b. World War II.

c. the Korean war.

d. the Vietnam war.

15. The most frequent residual symptom reported by combat veterans in a five-year follow up by De Fazio et al. (1975) was

a. difficulties with emotional closeness.

b. employment nightmares.

c. frequent nightmares.

d. being a "hothead."

6

Anxiety-based disorders (neuroses)

OVERVIEW

This chapter covers several behavior patterns that had, in the past, been called *neuroses*. Recently, however, the psychiatrists in charge of writing the classification of mental disorders (DSM–III) decided that *neurosis* was too broad a term and had entered everyday language where it was frequently misused. Therefore, the terms *anxiety, somatoform,* and *dissociative disorders* were substituted in DSM–III. These disorders are usually of mild to moderate intensity and seem to be related to faulty learning of anxiety-avoidance methods. In most cases, the disorders are episodic in nature with dramatic symptoms occurring only during periods of high stress. However, in between flare-ups of symptoms, these individuals are less happy and less effective than they could be if they learned more appropriate coping behavior. Individuals with these disorders respond well to psychotherapy or behavior therapy and rarely require hospitalization.

The chapter also contains a detailed description of the clinical picture, causal pattern, and treatment of the anxiety, somatoform, and dissociative disorders.

TERMS YOU SHOULD KNOW

neurosis (p. 187)

neurotic process (p. 188)

anxiety (p. 187)

neurotic paradox (p. 189)

neurotic style (p. 190)

inhibited behavior system (p. 191)

free-floating anxiety (p. 195)

anxiety disorder (p. 195)

anxiety attack (p. 195)

panic disorder (p. 195)

obsession (p. 199)

compulsion (p. 199)

phobia (p. 204)

somatoform disorder (p. 207)

somatization disorder (p. 207)

hypochondriasis (pp. 207–208)

psychogenic pain disorder (p. 210)

pain cocktail (p. 212)

conversion disorder (p. 212)

astasia-abasia (p. 215)

aphonia (p. 215)

mutism (p. 215)

belle indifference (p. 215)

malingering (p. 216)

dissociative disorder (p. 217)

amnesia (p. 217)

psychogenic amnesia (p. 217)

fugue state (p. 218)

multiple personality (p. 220)

coconscious personality (p. 220)

depersonalization (p. 222)

anxiety-defense (p. 224)

preparedness (p. 224)

meta-analysis (p. 226)

electrosleep (p. 226)

biofeedback-induced muscle relaxation (p. 226)

individual psychotherapy (p. 226)

behavior therapy (p. 227)

cognitive mediation (p. 228)

multimodal therapy (p. 229)

CONCEPTS TO MASTER

1. Introduction
    a. What was the original meaning of the term *neurosis* as introduced by Englishman William Cullen? (p. 187)

    b. How was the meaning of the term changed by Freud's theorizing? (p. 187)

    c. How has the term been further changed in recent years? (pp. 187–188)

    d. How many Americans are thought to possess neurotic symptoms? (p. 187)

    e. Why was the term *neurosis* avoided in the DSM–III? (p. 188)

    f. What are the three specific categories in DSM–III that take the place of the older, general category of neurosis? (p. 188)
        1.

        2.

        3.

    g. The neurotic process has at its core a special form of fear response called _____ along with inadequate coping abilities to control the feelings. (p. 188)

2. Neurotic anxiety
    a. Freud considered _____ to be the central problem in the neuroses. (p. 188)
    b. Compare and contrast fear and anxiety. (p. 188)

70

3. Neurotic paradox
   a. Neurotic individuals have the tendency to experience exceptional anxiety. What happens as a
      result of these high anxiety levels?   (p. 189)
      1. In perception of everyday situations?   (p. 189)

      2. In interpersonal relationships?   (p. 189)

      3. In energy level?   (p. 189)

   b. How is neurotic behavior a paradox?   (p. 190)

4. Neurotic styles
   a. A neurotic style is a _____ way of coping with anxiety.   (p. 190)
   b. The authors discuss a child born to parents who do not tolerate aggressive behavior in any form.
      If the child learns to respond with anxiety to all manifestations of aggressive behavior, he/she
      can be said to illustrate an _____ behavior system. As a consequence
      the individual can be expected to behave inappropriately in situations calling for some degree
      of aggression or assertion. How can the individual be expected to behave?   (pp. 191–192)

      Even if the individual does not act aggressively, can he/she be expected to experience
      anxiety?   (p. 192)

   c. Complete the following chart that summarizes inhibited behavior systems and the neurotic
      symptoms that may be associated with them if the individual experiences stress.   (pp. 192–194)

Inhibited Behavior System	Description	Neurotic Symptoms
aggression/assertion inhibition		hypertension, compulsive behavior
	individuals deny impulses to comply or submit.	defiance, noncompliance, dangerous risk taking
responsibility-independence inhibition		agoraphobia
	individuals experience unusual anxiety over forming close attachments.	

5. Anxiety disorders
   a. Anxiety disorders are characterized by the individual actually experiencing anxiety or by evidence of efforts to avoid anxiety. There are two basic forms of anxiety disorders: anxiety states and phobic disorder. Anxiety states include four subtypes.   (p. 195)
      1.

      2.

      3.

      4.

   b. Anxiety disorders are thought to affect _____ percent of the general population.
                                                                                          (p. 195)

6. Generalized anxiety disorders
   a. Generalized anxiety disorders are characterized by chronic anxiety of at least one month duration that does not appear to stem from any particular cause. This type of anxiety is referred to as _____ anxiety.   (p. 195)
   b. Describe the symptoms characteristic of individuals suffering from generalized anxiety disorder.
                                                                                          (p. 195)

    c.   How do the symptoms of panic disorder differ from generalized anxiety disorder?   (pp. 195–196)

7. Obsessive-compulsive disorder
    a.   What is the incidence of obsessive-compulsive disorder?   (p. 199)

    b.   What content is particularly common for obsessive thoughts to involve?   (p. 199)

    c.   What happens if a person with obsessive-compulsive disorder is prevented from performing the compulsive act?   (p. 202)

    d.   Why is obsessive-compulsive behavior considered maladaptive?   (p. 202)

    e.   A large proportion of obsessive-compulsive individuals are found to be unusually preoccupied with issues of _____ but may also involve aggression/assertion inhibition.   (p. 203)

8. Phobic disorder
    a.   What proportion of the population surveyed in Vermont was found to have phobias?   (p. 204)

        What proportion was found to have *severe* and *disabling* phobias?   (p. 204)

    b.   Circle the groups with the higher rates of phobias.
        men   or   women
        adolescents   or   older people
    c.   If a phobic person attempts to approach the object of his or her phobia, what happens?   (pp. 204–205)

    d.   What types of symptoms can phobic individuals show in addition to their phobias?   (p. 205)

e. Phobias are reinforced in two ways. What are they? (p. 205)

f. Over the years what happens to established phobias? (p. 207)

9. Somatization disorder
   a. Somatization disorder is suspected in a woman who presents _____
      physical complaints to the physician. (p. 207)
   b. How is somatization disorder differentiated from hypochondriasis? (p. 207)

10. Hypochondriasis
    a. What are the characteristic symptoms of hypochondriasis? (pp. 207–208)

    b. How can a hypochondriac be differentiated from the truly ill? (p. 208)

    c. The authors state that hypochondriasis can be viewed as an interpersonal strategy. What is
       the hypochondriac trying to say? (p. 210)

11. Psychogenic pain disorder
    a. Many physchogenic pain sufferers eventually end up truly disabled. How does this result
       occur? (p. 210)

    b. Do psychogenic pain disorders usually have any physiological damage to which they
       can be traced? (p. 210)

12. Conversion disorder
    a. Compared to the higher incidences in the past, how frequent are conversion disorders
       today? (p. 213)

    b. Why are these disorders decreasing in frequency? (p. 213)

c. Is it true that persons with hysterical deafness really cannot hear? (p. 215)

d. What is the most common conversion disorder of speech? (p. 215)

e. The authors discuss four ways in which conversion symptoms differ from actual physical illnesses. What are these? (pp. 215–216)
    1.

    2.

    3.

    4.

f. How can you distinguish a person with conversion symptoms from a person who is consciously faking an illness (i.e., a malingerer)? (p. 216)

g. Place the following events in the development of a conversion disorder in the proper causal sequence: (p. 216)
    1. under continued stress, the symptoms of illness appear.
    2. a desire to escape an unpleasant situation.
    3. a wish to be sick to avoid the situation.

    _____ ⟶
    _____ ⟶
    _____

h. What determines the particular symptoms the person prone to conversion disorder will develop? (p. 216)

i. What types of personality characteristics has the person prone to conversion disorder been found to have? (p. 216)

j. Are the following statements true or false?
   1. Enacting a sick role is only useful in some cultures, namely those that provide sympathy
       and support for sick persons.   (p. 217)
                                                                              True   False
   2. Conversion symptoms are modeled on whatever information about physical ailments the
       patient has.   (p. 217)
                                                                              True   False
   3. A sick role tends to be self-perpetuating.   (p. 217)
                                                                              True   False
k. Can a conversion reaction occur after an accident in which the victim hopes to obtain
    compensation?   (p. 217)

13. Dissociative disorders
    a. How are dissociative disorders like somatoform disorders?   (p. 217)

    b. The dissociative disorders consist of four different patterns. What are they?
        1.

        2.

        3.

        4.

    c. Label the following descriptions using the following terms: amnesia, localized amnesia,
        selective amnesia, generalized amnesia.   (p. 217)

        _____   In this form of amnesia, there is an actual failure of
                                            memory storage (i.e., retention). The memory somehow
                                            became truly lost.
        _____   In this form of amnesia, the individual forgets some but
                                            not all of what happened during a given period.
        _____   In this form of amnesia, an individual cannot recall
                                            events during the first few hours following a traumatic
                                            event.
        _____   In this form of amnesia, the individual forgets his or her
                                            entire life history.

    d. Psychogenic amnesia is highly selective. What type of material is most likely to be for-
        gotten?   (p. 217)

    e. How is amnesia like a conversion reaction?   (p. 218)

f. Kiersch (1962) found the _____ percent of amnesia cases among military personnel were due to deliberate suppression of memories. (p. 218)

g. What type of individual is most likely to develop amnesia in the face of conflict or stress? (p. 218)

h. How does the behavior during the fugue state compare to a person's previous personality? (p. 218)

14. Multiple personality
a. Multiple personality is a dissociative reaction, usually due to stress, in which the individual manifests two usually dramatically different _____. (p. 220)
b. How are "deep-seated conflicts between contradictory impulses and beliefs" involved as a causal factor in multiple personality? (p. 220)

c. Some researchers do not believe that multiple personalities really exist. What evidence do such researchers use to support their position? (p. 222)

15. Depersonalization disorder
a. Depersonalization occurs primarily among adolescents and young adults and involves a loss of _____. (p. 222)
b. In between episodes, individuals function normally except for anxiety and fear of
_____. (pp. 222–223)

16. Development and maintenance of neurotic behaviors
a. Pollin et al. (1969) studies the concordance rates of neurotic behavior among identical and fraternal twins in the military. What did they find? Did they conclude that their results supported genetic causation of neurosis? (p. 223)

b. The following are possible biological causes of neurosis. Check those areas that appear promising avenues of research. (p. 223)
   1. sex
   2. age
   3. glandular functioning
   4. loss of conditioning
   5. autonomic lability.
c. What model of the etiology of neuroses does the following diagram illustrate? (p. 224)

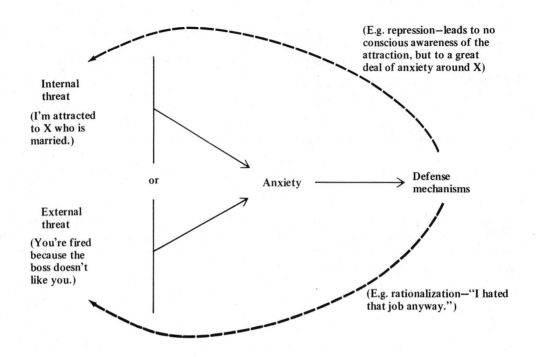

(E.g. repression—leads to no conscious awareness of the attraction, but to a great deal of anxiety around X)

Internal threat

(I'm attracted to X who is married.)

or

Anxiety ⟶ Defense mechanisms

External threat

(You're fired because the boss doesn't like you.)

(E.g. rationalization—"I hated that job anyway.")

d. Following are the four general psychosocial causes of neurotic behavior listed by the authors. Describe how each cause could contribute to the development of neurotic behavior.
   1. anxiety defense   (p. 224)

   2. faulty learning   (p. 224)

   3. blocked personal growth   (pp. 224–225)

   4. pathogenic interpersonal relationships.   (p. 225)

e. Describe the neurotic behavior found relatively more frequently among   (p. 225)
   1. Upper-class persons

   2. Lower-class persons.

78

17. Treatment and outcomes
    a. How much better off is the average neurotic who has received psychotherapy compared to neurotics who haven't received treatment? (p. 226)

    b. How many neurotic patients obtain symptom relief from drugs? (p. 226)

       What are the side effects of drugs? (p. 226)

       What can happen if neurotic symptoms are masked by drugs? (p. 226)

    c. Describe the objectives of the following psychological therapies for neurosis:
       1. individual psychotherapy (pp. 226–227)

       2. behavior therapy (p. 227)

       3. family therapy (p. 229)

       4. multimodal therapy (pp. 229–230)

    d. What problems can interfere with accomplishing the objectives of individual psychotherapy? Describe each of the behavioral treatment methods. (pp. 226–227)

    e. Which is the most common behavioral therapy method for neurosis? (pp. 227–228)
       1. systematic desensitization
       2. cognitive mediation
       Behavior therapy, although directed toward a specific focus, often has far reaching results. Explain. (p. 228)

f.   Indicate the percentage of neurotic persons who:

_____ percent benefit from psychotherapy for neurotic behavior.   (p. 230)

_____ percent decompensate into psychosis.   (p. 230)

(18.)   Neurasthenic disorder

a.   What is the principal complaint of persons diagnosed with this disorder?   (p. 208)

b.   What type of individuals characteristically develop it?   (p. 208)

c.   What is the prognosis?   (p. 209)

(19.)   Conversion reactions in student naval aviators

a.   What did Mucha and Reinhart do?   (p. 214)

b.   What were the background characteristics of their subjects?   (p. 214)

c.   What three factors did these researchers emphasize to account for the development of conversion symptoms among these subjects?   (p. 214)

1.

2.

3.

(20.)   Treatment of a patient with multiple phobias by a densensitization technique using imagery

a.   An "implosion technique" was used in this case. What is involved in implosion treatment?   (pp. 228–229)

b.   What are two alternate views of the type of learning that may be occurring in implosion?   (pp. 228–229)

1. The term _____ describes the observation that neurotic behavior persists although it is maladaptive in the long run.
   a. neurotic process
   b. neurotic nucleus
   c. neurotic paradox
   d. neurotic anxiety
2. Which of the following neurotic styles is most often associated with compulsive behavior?
   a. aggression/assertion
   b. compliance/submission
   c. responsibility/independence
   d. intimacy/trust
3. Which of the following is characterized primarily by free-floating anxiety?
   a. phobic disorder
   b. panic disorder
   c. generalized anxiety disorder
   d. post-traumatic stress disorder
4. Which of the following statements regarding obsessive-compulsive disorder is *false?*
   a. Obsessive thoughts are usually not carried out in action.
   b. The performance of a compulsive act usually brings increased tension.
   c. Obsessive-compulsive individuals are preoccupied with control.
   d. Obsessive-compulsive individuals are often perfectionists.
5. Which of the following statements is *false?*
   a. Phobic disorders occur more commonly among older rather than young adults.
   b. Phobias associated with phobic disorder interfere with everyday functioning.
   c. Phobic individuals have a wide range of symptoms other than fears.
   d. Phobias are influenced by cultural factors.
6. Which of the following is characterized by a multiplicity of physical complaints not restricted to any coherent symptom pattern and unrealistic fears of disease?
   a. somatization disorder
   b. hypochondriasis
   c. psychogenic pain disorder
   d. conversion reaction
7. Aphonia is
   a. inability to speak.
   b. ability to talk only in a whisper.
   c. a grotesque, disorganized walk.
   d. pseudopregnancy.
8. Belle indifference would be expected in cases of
   a. malingering.
   b. hypochondriases.
   c. conversion disorder.
   d. psychogenic pain disorder.
9. Which of the following statements is *false* regarding a paralysis diagnosed as conversion disorder?
   a. Little or no atrophy would be seen.
   b. The paralyzed limb might move during some activities.

c. The paralysis would probably disappear under hypnosis.

d. The paralysis would be viewed by the patient with anxiety, fear, and anger.

10. In _____ amnesia, the individual forgets his/her entire life history.

    a. localized

    b. selective

    c. generalized

    d. continuous

11. Two or more complete personalities are seen in

    a. fugue state.

    b. multiple personality.

    c. psychogenic amnesia.

    d. schizophrenia.

12. All of the following represent conclusions drawn by Pollen et al. (1969) in their study of neurosis in the military *except:*

    a. the concordance rate for neurosis is 1½ times higher among identical versus fraternal twins.

    b. the environmental background of identical twins was more similar than those of fraternal twins.

    c. heredity plays a minor role in the development of neurotic behavior.

    d. physiological factors are promising areas of research into the etiology of neurosis.

13. Which of the following accurately represents the sequence of events that leads to neurosis according to Frued?

    a. Threat ⟶ anxiety ⟶ defense mechanisms ⟶ maladaptive behavior.

    b. Anxiety ⟶ threat ⟶ defense mechanisms ⟶ maladaptive behavior.

    c. Maladaptive behavior ⟶ anxiety ⟶ threat ⟶ defense mechanisms.

    d. Defense mechanisms ⟶ anxiety ⟶ threat ⟶ maladaptive behavior.

14. Which group is relatively more likely to develop anxiety disorders?

    a. Australian aborigines

    b. middle-class Americans

    c. lower-class Americans

    d. gypsies

15. The most frequently used behavioral method in the treatment of neurosis is

    a. electrosleep.

    b. biofeedback-induced muscle relaxation.

    c. systematic desensitization.

    d. extinction.

7

Personality disorders and crime

OVERVIEW

In this chapter several specific disorders of personality are discussed. With these disorders we encounter, for the first time, behavior that is not episodic and that, generally, is not exacerbated by stress. Rather, the personality disorders represent ingrained "life-styles" or characteristic patterns that are maladaptive of meeting the individual's needs. Often, the person with a personality disorder ends up imposing on other people's rights in order to obtain his or her goals. Many individuals involved in criminal activity, although not all, are of this type.

Chapter 7 begins with descriptions of the various types of personality disorders, their causal patterns, and their treatment. The chapter concludes with a discussion of criminal behavior and approaches to dealing with criminals.

TERMS YOU SHOULD KNOW

personality

personality disorder (p. 233)

acting-out (p. 233)

paranoid personality (p. 237)

schizoid personality (p. 238)

schizotypal personality (p. 239)

histrionic personality (p. 239)

narcissistic personality (p. 240)

borderline personality (p. 241)

CONCEPTS TO MASTER

1. Introduction
   a. Tension and defense mechanisms are important in understanding neurosis disorders. Are they related to the development of the personality disorders? (p. 233)

   b. In general, what maladaptive behaviors characterize the person with a personality disorder? (p. 233)

   c. Why is the prevalence of personality disorders unknown? (p. 234)

   d. The formal definition of personality disorders is as follows: personality traits are enduring patterns of _____. Only when personality traits become inflexible and cause social and occupational impairment or subjective distress is personality disorder diagnosed. Personality disorders are recognizable by _____, and last throughout adult life. Personality disorders are continuous not discrete periods of illness. (p. 234)
   e. Why are personality disorders diagnosed on Axis II of DSM–III? (p. 235)

84

f.   Why does a great deal of misuse of diagnostic labels occur with the personality disorders? (The authors list three problems that account for the misuse.)   (pp. 234–235)

   1.

   2.

   3.

2.   Clinical features of personality disorders

   a.   Persons with personality disorders have several features in common. Describe the characteristic behavior of personality disordered people in each of the following general areas:

      1.   personal relationships   (p. 236)

      2.   duration of difficulties   (p. 236)

      3.   flexibility of behavior in various situations   (pp. 236–237)

      4.   motivation for change through psychotherapy.   (p. 237)

3.   Types of personality disorders

   a.   List the personality disorders that belong to each cluster.   (p. 237)

      1.   Cluster I: odd or eccentric individuals

      2.   Cluster II: dramatic, emotional individuals

      3.   Cluster III: anxious, fearful individuals

b. Fill in the clinical picture in the following personality disorders.

Personality Disorder	Description
paranoid (p. 237)	
schizoid (p. 238)	
schizotypal (p. 239)	
histrionic (p. 239)	
narcissistic (p. 240)	
borderline (p. 241)	
avoidant (p. 242)	
dependent (p. 242)	
compulsive (p. 243)	
passive-aggressive (p. 244)	

4. Causal factors in personality disorder
   a. Why hasn't the study of causal factors of personality disorders progressed
       very far?   (pp. 244–245)

   b. What is the current status of theories that link physique or constitutional reaction tendencies
       to the development of personality disorders?   (p. 245)

   c. What is the current status of theories that attempt to link psychosocial factors to the
       development of personality disorders?   (p. 245)

d. What is the current status of theories that attempt to link our society's high value on impulse gratification, instant solutions, etc. to the development of personality disorders? (p. 245)

5. Treatment and outcome
    a. What is the generally accepted prognosis for persons with personality disorders? (p. 245)

    b. Under what circumstances do persons with personality disorders generally get involved with psychotherapy? (p. 245)

    c. How do the difficulties personality disordered people have with personal relationships, acting out, and avoiding problems affect the course of psychotherapeutic treatments? (p. 246)

    d. Why is psychotherapy for personality disorders more likely to be effective in situations like prisons? (p. 247)

6. Antisocial (psychopathic) personality
    a. What is the incidence of antisocial personality in United States males? (p. 248)

        In United States females? (p. 248)

    b. What is the typical age of onset for antisocial personality in males? (p. 248)

        In females? (p. 248)

7. Clinical picture in antisocial personality
    a. The DSM–III classification of antisocial personality involves the following criteria. (p. 248)
        1. _____ instances of deviant behavior before age _____.
        2. Four behavior problems such as _____ since age 15.
        3. No remission since age 15.
        4. No mental disorder that could cause the symptoms.
    b. Fill in the missing information on the following chart that summarizes the personality characteristics of antisocial persons.

Area of Functioning	Behavior Typical of the Antisocial Person
1. conscience development (p. 248)	
2. feelings of anxiety and guilt (p. 248)	
3. impulse control (p. 249)	
4. frustration tolerance (p. 249)	
5. ability to accept authority (p. 249)	
6. ability to accept responsibility and profit from experience (p. 249)	
7. interpersonal (including sexual) relationships (p. 249)	
8. ability to impress and manipulate others (p. 250)	

8. Causal factors in antisocial personality
   a. The authors cite the following three constitutional factors as possible causes of antisocial personality disorder. Respond to the following question regarding these factors.
      1. Malfunction of inhibitory mechanisms
         What is the likelihood that abnormalities of neural functioning as reflected by EEG patterns are a major causal factor in antisocial personality? (p. 253)

2. Deficient emotional arousal
   Many investigators—e.g., Lykken (1957), Eysenck (1950), Hare (1970)—have found that antisocial individuals seem to lack normal fear and anxiety reactions. What appears to happen in the development of antisocial persons as a result of their lack of anxiety and fear? (p. 253)

   Schmauk (1970) found that antisocial persons can learn to avoid punishment only if the punishment is meaningful to them. Which of the following punishments did he find was effective with antisocial persons: physical punishment (electric shock), social punishment ("That was a very dumb thing to do."), or loss of money? (p. 253)

   Describe Valliant's view regarding antisocial individual's handling of anxiety. (pp. 253–254)

3. Stimulation seeking
   Hare (1968) reported that antisocial individuals were deficient in autonomic variability. What do such individuals do to attempt to compensate for this deficit according to Quay (1965)? (p. 254)

b. The authors state that three types of family relationships may be causally related to anti-social personality. Respond to the following questions regarding these factors.
   1. Early parental loss
      Although the loss of a parent during childhood was more common among antisocial subjects than normal controls, the authors of the text conclude that this factor can only be a partial or interactive cause of antisocial personality. On what evidence do they base this conclusion? (p. 254)

   2. Parental rejection and inconsistency
      McCord and McCord (1964) concluded that severe _____ by parents was a primary cause of antisocial personality. (p. 254)
      Buss (1966), on the other hand, states that there are two parental patterns that account for development of antisocial personality. What are these two types? (p. 255)

1.

2.

3. Faulty parental models
   What type of parental behavior was seen by Greenacre (1945) in his study of antisocial persons from middle-class families? Thus, is modeling important in the development of antisocial behavior? (pp. 255–256)

c. The authors also highlight the role of sociocultural factors in the causation of antisocial personality.
   What factors in our urban ghettos may foster the development of antisocial behavior in youngsters who grow up in such areas? (pp. 256–257)

9. Treatment and outcomes
   a. Bandura (1969) has suggested a treatment program to modify antisocial behavior through the application of learning principles. Briefly summarize the three components of this treatment. (p. 258)
      1.

      2.

      3.

   b. Is psychotherapy with antisocial persons usually successful when attempted on an outpatient basis? (p. 258)

      Is one-to-one, as opposed to group, therapy usually effective? (p. 258)

c. Why do many antisocial persons seem to improve after age 40? (p. 258)

10. Incidence (of crime)
    a. Has crime really been on the rise from 1972 to 1981? (p. 259)

    b. The problem of crime is probably even more serious than the figures indicate, since anywhere from _____ to _____ % of all crimes are not reported to the police. (p. 259)
    c. Approximately _____ percent of all criminals are male. (p. 259)
    d. Place the following in the appropriate column, indicating whether they are characterized by relatively high or low rates of crime: (p. 259)
       metropolitan areas
       rural areas
       West (part of the United States)
       Northwest (part of the United States)
       South (part of the United States)
       low socioeconomic persons
       males
       persons under eighteen
       blacks
       women.

Relatively Lower Crime Rates	Relatively Higher Crime Rates

11. Causal factors in criminal behavior
    a. What characteristics are typical of the man with XYY chromosomal makeup? How frequent is this chromosomal make-up according to Jarvik et al. (1973). (p. 260)

What is the current status of the XXY explanation of criminal behavior according to Witkin et al. (1976)? (p. 261)

b. Is abnormal neural functioning as reflected by EEGs thought to be related to participation in criminal activity? (p. 261)

c. On the whole, about _____ of sentenced prisoners could be regarded as psychiatric cases. (p. 261)
Three forms of psychopathology seem to be the most common among criminals. They are: (p. 261)
1.

2.

3.

d. Is severe life stress thought to play any role in the triggering of impulsive acts of violence and other antisocial behavior? (p. 261)

e. What is the relationship of social class and criminality in Danish studies? (p. 262)

f. Discuss how criminality could be fostered by (pp. 262–263)
1. television

2. attitudes.

g. Describe the following types of criminals:
1. "professional" criminal (p. 265)

2. "organized" criminal (p. 265)

3. "thrill-seeking" criminal   (p. 266)

4. "loser" criminal.   (p. 266)

12. Approaches to dealing with criminals
    a. There are three traditional purposes of punishment of criminals: revenge by society, protection
       of society, and deterrence (prevention of future crime by the offender and others). How
       well does the prison system protect society?   (p. 267)

       How well does it deter crime?

       What three factors limit the deterrent effects of the prison system?   (p. 267)
       1.

       2.

       3.

    b. "Indeterminate sentencing" means that a prisoner will remain in jail until the prison staff feels
       he or she is rehabilitated. It was thought that this type of sentencing would result in shorter
       prison sentences and facilitate return to the community. What actually happened? (p. 268)

    c. Are there any treatment techniques in rehabilitating criminals that are predictably effective as
       well as socially acceptable?   (p. 268)

    d. Do the authors of the text want to see more large prisons such as Attica or San Quentin
       built?   (p. 270)

    e. Answer true or false to the following statements to reflect the views of the authors:
       1. No rehabilitation methods have been found that are both effective and ethical. true or false
                                                                               (pp. 269–270)
       2. Criminals should be given indeterminate sentences.   true or false   (p. 270)

93

3. Prisons should be smaller. (p. 270)
4. Correctional personnel should be required to meet certain standards. (p. 270)
f. Describe the characteristics of the "violent predator." (p. 270)

(13.) Facts about homicide
a. What is the difference between first-degree murder, second-degree murder, and manslaughter? (p. 262)

b. What proportion of murders involve a victim and an offender who are close relatives or friends? (p. 262)

c. What proportion of murders involve firearms? (p. 263)

CHAPTER QUIZ

1. Personality disorders are
   a. reactions to stress.
   b. intrapsychic disturbances.
   c. episodic in nature.
   d. maladaptive ways of perceiving, thinking, and relating.
2. Personality disorders are coded on Axis _____ of DSM–III.
   a. I
   b. II
   c. III
   d. IV
3. Diagnosis of personality disorders is difficult for all the following reasons *except*
   a. their diagnosis requires inference rather than observation.
   b. they blend into normal ranges of behavior.
   c. the criteria are mutually exclusive.
   d. they are poorly understood.
4. Which of the following belongs in the cluster of personality disorders characterized by anxiety?
   a. avoidant
   b. schizotypal
   c. schizoid
   d. paranoid
5. Individuals with this personality disorder typically show oddities of thought, perception or speech:
   a. schizoid.
   b. shizotypal.

    c. histrionic.

    d. antisocial.

6. David, the 29-year-old "great procrastinator," is an example of _____ personality disorder.

    a. passive-aggressive

    b. avoidant

    c. narcissistic

    d. borderline

7. Establishing the causal factors of personality disorders hasn't progressed very far for all the following reasons except

    a. the behaviors of interest blend into the normal range.

    b. affected individuals do not seek professional help.

    c. the personality disorders weren't recognized before 1952.

    d. only retrospective studies have been possible so far.

8. Which of the following factors has been largely eliminated as a cause of personality disorder?

    a. early learning

    b. constitutional reaction tendencies

    c. societal values

    d. genetic factors

9. Which of the following statements regarding psychotherapy with a personality disordered client is *untrue?*

    a. Individual therapy is usually more effective than group therapy.

    b. Personality disordered client is usually seen as part of another person's treatment.

    c. Client deals with his/her problems not verbally but through acting out.

    d. This type of client is usually thought to be resistant to treatment.

10. A 25-year-old man had repeated scrapes with the law when he was 12–18 years old. He is impulsive, financially irresponsible, and drinks excessively although he hasn't been in trouble with the law as an adult. Would he be properly diagnosed "antisocial personality?"

    a. Yes.

    b. No.

    c. Depends on work history.

    d. Depends on whether he has had any five years free from the problems described.

11. Antisocial persons are rarely rehabilitated in prison. This failure is related to all the following except

    a. inability to maintain good interpersonal relationships.

    b. inability to profit from experience.

    c. rejection of authority.

    d. inadequate conscience development.

12. Studying the EEGs of antisocial persons by Hare (1970) revealed

    a. deficient emotional arousal.

    b. decreased sensitivity to noxious stimuli.

    c. malfunction of inhibitory mechanisms.

    d. failure to respond to punishment.

13. All of the following can often foster the development of antisocial personality disorder *except*

    a. early parental loss.

    b. cold, distant parents.

    c. inconsistent, capricious parents.

    d. middle-class parents who emphasize appearances.

14. Treatment of the antisocial person according to Bandura (1969) requires all of the following *except*
    a. withdrawal of meaningful reinforcements for disapproved behavior.
    b. modeling of desired behavior.
    c. transition from material rewards to self-rewards.
    d. strengthening of external controls.
15. Men who commit the crime of rape have been viewed as having _____ that caused their behavior.
    a. an XYY genetic makeup
    b. low forehead and unusually shaped jaw
    c. brain damage and mental retardation
    d. deviant attitudes.

8

Psychological factors and physical illness

OVERVIEW

The theme of stress that has been discussed in previous chapters also occupies a central position in this chapter on physical disease. The chapter presents the view that all physical disease is related to stress to some degree. At one end of the continuum are diseases, such as viral meningitis, that are primarily due to the invasion of body cells by a potent virus. However, the degree of stress a person is experiencing influences the efficiency with which the individual resists the virus and how rapidly he or she recovers. At the other end of the continuum are diseases, such as peptic ulcers, that mainly represent the direct results of stress overload. This type of disease would not be seen in an individual unless high levels of stress were present.

Chapter 8 first discusses the relationship of stress, the autonomic nervous system, and health. Then, specific data on the clinical picture and treatment of such diseases as peptic ulcers, anorexia nervosa, migraine headaches, hypertension, and heart attacks are reviewed.

TERMS YOU SHOULD KNOW

behavioral medicine (p. 273)

psychogenic (p. 273)

health psychology (p. 273)

psychophysiologic disorders (p. 274)

placebo effect (p. 275)

adrenal medulla (p. 276)

adrenal cortex (p. 276)

glucocorticoids (p. 277)

phasic (p. 278)

peptic ulcer (p. 279)

anorexia nervosa (p. 280)

pre-anorexic state (p. 281)

migraine headache (p. 282)

unilateral headaches (p. 282)

hypertension (p. 284)

essential hypertension (p. 284)

coronary heart disease (p. 285)

Type-A person (p. 286)

asthma (p. 287)

autonomic reactivity (p. 288)

somatic weakness (p. 288)

corticovisceral control mechanisms (p. 288)

broken heart syndrome (p. 290)

secondary gain (p. 291)

electrosleep (p. 293)

morita therapy (p. 293)

biofeedback (p. 294)

CONCEPTS TO MASTER

1. Introduction
    a. What did Flanders Dunbar mean by the statement that it is "more important to know what kind of patient has the disease than to know what kind of disease the patient has"? (p. 274)

    b. How are psychophysiological disorders categorized in DSM–III? (p. 274)

2. Emotions and health
   a. What has been learned by researchers such as Rahe (1974), Payne (1975), and Brown (1972) about the likelihood of illness under increasing levels of stress?   (p. 275)

   b. Why is it important for a cancer patient, for example, to believe in his or her doctor, to have faith in the treatment, and to have an overall positive mental outlook?   (p. 275)

3. Autonomic excess and classic psychophysiologic illness   (p. 276)
   a. Place the following terms in their proper order according to F. Alexander's theory:
      1. strong emotions (conscious or unconscious)
      2. unrealistic fears and anxieties
      3. defensive and self-defeating strategies.

      _____ ⟶ _____ ⟶ _____ ⟶ psychophysiologic disorders

4. Selye and the stress-response system
   a. Under severe stress the cortex of the adrenal gland releases glucocorticoids into the bloodstream. Listed below are several bodily responses. Use a " + " to indicate that the glucocorticoids enhance the response and a " − " to indicate that they hamper the response.   (p. 277)

Effects of Glucocorticoids

Bodily Response	**Effect**
1. amount of blood sugar	_____
2. blood redistribution	_____
3. control of tissue damage	_____
4. resistance to infection	_____
5. number of circulating white blood cells	_____
6. rate of bodily growth	_____
7. amount of sexual and reproductive hormones	_____

   b. Stress may serve as a predisposing, precipitating, or reinforcing factor in the causal pattern of psychophysiologic disorders. True or false?   (p. 277)
      Stress can speed up the onset of disease, increase its severity, and interfere with the body's resistance to disease. True or false?   (p. 277)

5. Life-style as an added factor in health maintenance
   a. Habits under an individual's control are believed to play a major causal role in the three major causes of death. True or false? (p. 277)
   b. The data between habits and disease is correlational. Why can't these data be considered conclusive proof? (p. 278)

6. Peptic ulcers
   a. How has the incidence of ulcers changed during the last century? (p. 279)

   b. What types of emotional states may stimulate the flow of gastric juices? (p. 279)

   c. Respond to the following questions regarding the research of Weiner et al. (1957).
      1. Who were the subjects in this study, and how were they divided into two groups? (p. 279)

      2. What did the researchers find? (p. 279)

      3. What were the three factors that all had to be present in order to "challenge the equilibrium" and produce an abnormally high ulcer risk? (p. 279)
         a.

         b.

         c.

7. Anorexia nervosa
   a. Once quite rare, the incidence of anorexia is now _____ percent of women aged 12–25. It occurs 20 times more frequently in women than men. (p. 280)
   b. Diagnosis of anorexia requires the presence of (pp. 280–281)
      1. onset before _____
      2. weight loss of more than _____ percent of original body weight
      3. distorted attitude toward _____
      4. no other medical illness
      5. no other psychiatric disorder
      6. at least two of the following six manifestations:

         _____

         _____

100

_____

_____

_____

_____

c. Describe the psychosocial characteristics of the typical anorexic according to Crisp et al. (1976).   (p. 281)

d. Describe when and how anorexia begins.   (p. 281)

8. Migraine and tension headaches
    a. How many Americans are believed to suffer from headaches?   (p. 282)

    b. What physiological change is associated with the onset of migraine headache pain?   (p. 282)

    c. Do stressors, such as frustrations, excessive performance demands, etc., cause cranial artery dilation in everyone?   (p. 282)

    d. What physiological changes lead to tension headaches?   (p. 283)

    e. When do headaches typically begin?   (p. 283)

    f. Do migraine sufferers differ from people who don't suffer from headaches in terms of psychological adjustment according to Andrasik et al. (1982)?   (p. 284)

9. Hypertension
    a. What changes in blood distribution take place when an individual is subjected to stress?   (p. 284)

b. Under what circumstances does high blood pressure become chronic?   (p. 284)

c. What percentage of Americans suffer from hypertension?   (p. 284)

What is the incidence among blacks as compared to whites?

d. Why is hypertension potentially serious?   (p. 284)

e. In what proportion of hypertension cases can organic causes be ruled out?   (p. 284)

f. Describe the "suppressed rage" hypothesis of hypertension.   (p. 285)

10. Coronary heart disease
     a. How do men and women compare in terms of vulnerability to heart attacks?   (p. 285)

     b. What degree of stress has been found during the final six months of the lives of heart attack victims?   (pp. 285–286)

     c. What factors were found to characterize the backgrounds of subjects who had recently survived myocardial infarctions in Finland, Sweden, and the United States?   (p. 286)

     d. Describe the Type-A person. Into what kind of a situation can Type-A convert ordinary life circumstances?   (p. 286)

     e. How much greater is the risk of heart attack for the Type-A male age 39–49 than for the Type-B male of the same age group?   (p. 286)

11. Other specific reaction patterns
    What evidence has cast doubt on a view of asthma as caused entirely by psychological
    factors? (p. 287)

12. General causes of psychophysiologic disorders
    a. What is the "problem of organ specificity"? (p. 287)

    b. The *primary* causal factor that underlies all psychophysiologic disorders is
    _____. (p. 287)

    c. Place the following events in the development of psychophysiologic disorders in their
       correct order: (p. 287)
       1. concentration of organ system response
       2. failure of emotions to be dealt with adequately
       3. arousal of negative emotions in response to stress.
       _____ ⟶ _____ ⟶ _____

13. Biological factors
    a. The authors discuss three general biological causal factors: genetic causes, differences in autonomic
       reactivity/somatic weakness, and disturbed corticovisceral control mechanisms. Respond to the
       following questions regarding each theory.
       1. Genetic causes
          What results have been found regarding the frequency of similar psychosomatic problems
          among members of the same family? (p. 288)

          What kinds of twins did Liljefors and Rahe (1970) study? What are the implications of
          their findings? (p. 288)

       2. Autonomic reactivity/somatic weakness
          What is a "stomach reactor"? (p. 288)

How early would such a pattern of response be developed? (p. 288)

If a stomach reactor were to develop a psychophysiologic condition, which one would it likely be? (p. 288)

What kinds of factors might lead an individual to develop a particular organ weakness? (p. 288)

3. Corticovisceral control disfunction
    Some individuals appear to have a deficiency in their hypothalamus that leads to over-stimulation of the pituitary that subsequently leads to overstimulation of the adrenal gland and, thus, to oversecretion of adrenocortical hormones. An excess of these hormones can cause an organism to function the majority of time as if it were under stress. The authors label this sequence of events an inadequate _____
    control mechanism. (p. 288)
    Hill et al. (1967) reported decreased lymphocyte production during periods of
    _____. (p. 289)

14. Psychosocial factors
    a. Respond to the following questions regarding the three major psychosocial causes of psycho-physiologic illness:
        1. Personality characteristics/coping patterns
            Dunbar thought that there were specific personality characteristics associated with particular psychophysiologic disorders. Recent research, such as Kidson's (1973) and Jenkins' (1974), has cast doubt on this view. What type of data did these two investigators produce? (p. 290)

            What has been found about the ability of many psychophysiologic patients to express their emotions? (p. 290)

            What has been found regarding the use of various defense mechanisms by psycho-physiologic patients? (p. 290)

104

What has been learned in experimental situations where subjects are purposely frustrated and then permitted physical or fantasy aggression? (p. 290)

2. Interpersonal relationships
   How is the incidence of illness related to the following?
   a. marital problems, divorce (Bloom et al., 1978) (p. 290)

   b. bereavement (Parkes et al., 1969) (p. 290)

   It has been found by Weiner et al. (1957) that frustrations of dependency needs combined with other factors (i.e., stress of basic training, physiological vulnerability in the form of high pepsinogen levels) leads to peptic ulcer formation. Have researchers been successful in linking any other specific stressor (such as dependency need frustration) to specific psychosomatic symptoms? (p. 290)

   What is the "broken heart syndrome"? (p. 290)

   Explain how the overprotectiveness and tendency to reject the child that has been observed in asthmatic children's mothers could just as easily be viewed as both a *cause* of the child's asthma and an *effect* of the child's asthma. (p. 291)

3. Autonomic learning
   It is now known that the autonomic responses that lead to psychophysiologic symptoms can be learned involuntarily through _____
   conditioning and voluntarily through _____
   conditioning. (p. 291)
   Psychophysiologic symptoms may be elicited through suggestion and maintained through reinforcement. The ability of suggestion in eliciting a psychosomatic symptom was demonstrated with asthmatics. How was this experiment done? (p. 291)

15. Sociocultural factors
    a. How common are psychophysiologic illnesses among underdeveloped peoples? (p. 291)

    b. In what socioeconomic class are psychophysiologic illnesses most common? (p. 292)

16. Treatment and outcomes—biological measures
    a. Treatment for psychophysiologic disorders begins with a thorough assessment of
    _____. (p. 292)
    Treatment is usually similar to that for _____. (p. 292)
    b. What can the use of drugs accomplish in the treatment of psychophysiologic
    disorders? (p. 292)

17. Psychosocial measures
    a. On what assumption is behavior therapy for psychophysiologic disorders based? (p. 293)

    b. How successful are relaxation techniques in the treatment of migraine headaches and hyper-
    tension? (p. 294)

    c. How was the success of biofeedback related to the severity of illness in the case of asthmatic
    children? (p. 294)

    d. How does biofeedback compare to simple relaxation training in terms of effectiveness? (p. 295)

    e. The _____ treatment approach can involve teaching
    clients stress management techniques. (p. 295)

18. Combined treatment measures
What factors does Leon believe must be addressed in a comprehensive treatment program
for anorexia? (p. 295)

19. Sociocultural measures
The North Karelia Project was aimed at reducing atherosclerotic disease in an entire Finnish
province. Describe the following aspects of the program:
1. overall goal (p. 296)

2. activities undertaken by project staff (p. 296)

3. early results. (pp. 296–297)

(20.) Biological clocks
What is a "circadian cycle?" (p. 289)

CHAPTER QUIZ

1. Health psychology deals with the diagnosis, treatment and prevention of
   a. anxiety disorders.
   b. physical disorders.
   c. stress disorders.
   d. psychogenic physical disorders.
2. A patient who shows improvement after a trusted physician gives him an injection of sterile water is
   demonstrating
   a. Hawthorne effect.
   b. placebo effect.
   c. demand characteristics.
   d. faith healing.
3. The person with a psychophysiologic illness has typically developed unrealistic
   a. vulnerabilities.
   b. defenses.
   c. frustrations.
   d. fears or anxieties.

4. In the stages of Seyle's stress response system, it is the _____ that is mainly involved.
   a. adrenal medulla
   b. autonomic nervous system
   c. adrenal cortex
   d. voluntary nervous system.
5. One of the effects of the glucocorticoids is to
   a. speed growth of new tissue.
   b. bolster formation of disease fighting antibodies.
   c. decrease production of growth and sex hormones.
   d. increase number of white blood cells.
6. Stress may play any of the following roles in the causal pattern of psychophysiologic disorders *except*
   a. primary.
   b. predisposing.
   c. precipitating.
   d. reinforcing.
7. Weiner's classic study of peptic ulcers involved monitoring the level of _____ among army draftees undergoing basic training.
   a. sex hormone
   b. glucocorticoids
   c. white blood cells
   d. pepsinogen
8. How common is anorexia nervosa among women 12–25?
   a. 0.5 percent
   b. 1 percent
   c. 5 percent
   d. 10 percent
9. Which of the following statements regarding the onset of anorexia is *false?*
   a. Onset is largely during adolesence.
   b. Onset is often connected to life tasks of which the person feels inadequate.
   c. Onset is often an extension of normal dieting.
   d. Onset is connected to a strong desire to achieve independent adulthood.
10. Dilation of the cranial arteries is associated with
    a. tension headaches.
    b. essential hypertension.
    c. migraine headaches.
    d. asthma.
11. Which of the following is *not* typical of persons who have experienced myocardial infarction (heart attack)?
    a. Heavy work responsibility.
    b. Type B personality.
    c. Time urgency.
    d. Hostility toward others.
12. Current thinking suggests that _____ is due more to innate physical vulnerability than to psychological factors.
    a. asthma
    b. migraine headaches

c. essential hypertension

d. peptic ulcer

13. The observation that immune function is decreased among recently bereaved individuals illustrates

    a. disruption of corticovisceral control mechanisms.

    b. somatic weakness.

    c. differences in autonomic reactivity.

    d. immune reactivity.

14. Which of the following personality characteristics is weakly but significantly correlated with the occurrence of psychophysiologic disorder?

    a. Insecure, anxious, sensitive.

    b. Impulsive, irresponsible.

    c. Withdrawn, uncommunicative.

    d. Funloving, energetic.

15. Which of the following statements regarding psychophysiologic symptoms is *false?*

    a. They can be conditioned voluntarily via classical conditioning.

    b. They may be learned through operant conditioning.

    c. They may be elicited by suggestion.

    d. They may be maintained by reinforcement.

9

Affective disorders and suicide

OVERVIEW

The disorders of mood—depression and mania—are discussed in this chapter. Depression is an extremely important topic, since it is the most common mood clinicians encounter among persons who seek psychological help. In addition, depression is extremely common among the normal population who do not seek the help of a professional mental health person but who do seek relief from family, friends, clergy, physicians, and, often, from bartenders or hairdressers. This section of the chapter begins with a differentiation of clinical depression from the normal depression many people experience. Then, the clinical picture of the different levels of severity of clinical depression are covered. The section concludes with a description of the causal pattern and treatment approaches to both depression and mania.

The second half of the chapter discusses suicide which is a risk with all depressed individuals.

Well-known persons periodically capture the headlines by killing themselves at the height of success and in the midst of lives of luxury and recognition. Often, they do not seem, from the outside, to have a bad life or many insolvable problems. These deaths mystify and disturb most of us and raise questions about what makes life livable (or unlivable). This section presents information relevant to these questions, asking, for instance, whether all persons who commit suicide are mentally disordered. Data are also presented on the increasing problem of suicide among young people and college students.

The section concludes with a discussion of some of the factors that characterize the person who is at high risk for suicide and a brief description of the procedures of suicide prevention.

TERMS YOU SHOULD KNOW

affective disorder (p. 299)

affect (p. 300)

mood congruent (p. 301)

CONCEPTS TO MASTER

1. Introduction
   a. The affective disorders are *primarily* disorders of _____, whereas schizophrenia and paranoia are *primarily* disorders of _____. (p. 300)
   b. The person who has an extreme affective disorder may have disturbed thinking, but, in contrast to schizophrenics, the thinking is often mood congruent. What does this statement mean?

Give an example. (pp. 300–301)

    c. Record the appropriate incidence information for major depression.
        1. _____ million Americans will be affected by major depression sometime during
            their life or _____ persons out of 100. (p. 301)
        2. The bulk of cases occur between ages _____. (p. 301)
        3. Females are affected considerably more often than males. (p. 301)
    d. How can depression be viewed as adaptive? (p. 302)

2. Normal depression
    a. Which is more common, "normal" or "abnormal" depression? (p. 302)

    b. What usually causes "normal depression"? (p. 302)

    c. Grief is a psychological process one goes through following the death of a loved one. It can be
        thought of as a normal depression. Describe the following symptoms of grief:
        1. turning-off on events (p. 302)

        2. fantasies. (p. 302)

    d. Clayton (1982) suggests that the normal length of the grieving process is
        _____. After this, therapeutic intervention is called for. (p. 303)
    e. What three psychological variables are involved in normal depression among college students
        according to Blatt et al. (1976)? (p. 303)
        1.

        2.

        3.

3. Mild to moderate affective disorders
    a. The three main affective disorders of mild to moderate severity recognized by DSM–III are
        cyclothymic disorder, dysthymic disorder, and adjustment disorder with depressed mood.
        Which of these describes
        1. nondisabling cyclical mood alterations between depression and elation? (p. 304)

2. nonpsychotic levels of depression lasting two years or more? (p. 305)

3. nonpsychotic level of depression developing within three months of an identifiable stressor? (p. 306)

4. Moderate to severe affective disorders
   a. Major depression (single episode or recurrent episodes) and bipolar disorder are the moderate to severe affective disorders. Respond to the following questions regarding their incidence and cause. The diagnosis of _____ cannot be (p. 308) made if the person has even one episode of manic behavior. Of people suffering from affective disorders, approximately _____ percent experience recurring episodes (pp. 308–309) according to Coryell and Winokur (1982). Each episode lasts an average of _____ months. In between episodes the individual may behave (p. 309) essentially normally, but this point hasn't been fully resolved. Approximately _____ percent of persons with major depression recover completely (p. 309) (have no episodes for five years). At all levels of severity, affective disorders are more prevalent among women than men by a ratio of _____. (p. 311)
   b. The clinical picture of major depressive disorder and bipolar disorder are compared in the following chart. Fill in the missing information.

Clinical Picture	Major Depression	Bipolar Depression
recurrent episodes	yes	yes
manic episodes	no	yes
age of onset	(p. 311)	25–30
duration of episodes	4 months	(p. 311)
number of recurrences	fewer	more
mortality from suicide	increased	greatly increased
probability of full recovery	40%	(p. 311)

   c. The symptoms of mania and depression are compared in the following chart. Fill in the missing information.

113

Area of Behavior	Depression	Mania
activity level	loss of interest in activities	(p. 310)
mood	(p. 308)	euphoric
mental activity	diminished cognitive capacity	flight of ideas
verbal output	reduced	(p. 310)
self-esteem	self-denunciation and guilt	(p. 310)
sleeping	hypersomnia or insomnia	(p. 310)

    d.   Indicate the points the authors of the text make related to schizoaffective disorder.
        1. What is a schizoaffective disorder? (p. 313)

        2. Does a disorder really exist in which the symptoms of affective psychosis and schizophrenia are mixed? (p. 313)

5. Biological factors
    a.   Three biological factors are thought to contribute to the development of affective disorders: hereditary predisposition, neurophysiological factors, and biochemical factors. Respond to the following questions regarding them.
        1. Hereditary predisposition
            The concordance rate for depression is much higher among identical than fraternal twins. Also, Slater (1944) reported that _____ percent of close relatives of "manic-depressives" (old name for bipolar affective disorder) were also affected compared to a rate of _____ percent. These findings could suggest a genetic basis for bipolar disorder. (p. 314)
            What have "adoption method" studies of bipolar disorder revealed? (p. 314)

            On what type of evidence is the "X-linkage hypothesis" of bipolar disorder based? (p. 315)

114

2. Neurophysiological factors
   What type of imbalance might lead to mood swings according to Pavlov?   (p. 315)

   What evidence supports this viewpoint?   (p. 315)

   How is the viewpoint simplistic?   (p. 315)

3. Biochemical factors
   Many therapies for affective disorders, such as ECT, lithium, and antidepressants, affect the level of "biogenic amines." What is the implication of this observation?   (p. 315)

b. The authors of the text state that the evidence that affective disorders involve a biological mechanism is compelling. They further state that this conclusion rests on "three facts that are beyond reasonable dispute." What are these three facts?   (p. 316)
   1.

   2.

   3.

6. Psychosocial factors
   a. The authors of the text present five categories of psychosocial factors that may influence the development of affective disorders: stress, personality characteristics, feelings of helplessness/loss of hope, defenses against stress, and interpersonal gains. Respond to the following questions regarding them.
      1. Stress
         How might stress affect the biochemistry of the brain, according to Barchas et al. (1967)?   (pp. 316–317)

Beck (1967) has listed six events that he believes are the most frequent aversive experiences occurring in the lives of people who become depressed. What are the first three of these?   (p. 317)

1.

2.

3.

How frequently do affective disorders occur spontaneously (endogenously) with no apparent precipitating event?   (p. 318)

2. Predisposing personality characteristics
   What does a "negative cognitive set" consist of?   (p. 319)

   How have the personality characteristics of adults who later suffer manic episodes been described?   (p. 319)

   How have the personality characteristics of adults who later suffer depressive episodes been described?   (p. 319)

3. Feelings of helplessness/loss of hope
   There are two explanations of depression that are based on learning theory. Briefly explain each one:
   a. "learned helplessness"—Seligman (1973 and 1975)   (p. 319)

b.   insufficient reinforcers—Lazarus, Lewinsohn (1968 and 1974).   (p. 320)

How has Ferster (1973) explained mania in learning theory terms?   (p. 320)

4. Defenses against stress
    How can mania be viewed as a defense against stress?   (p. 320)

    How can depression be viewed as a defense against stress?   (p. 321)

    Do the authors of the text believe it is wise to rely on psychological explanations of
    depression?   (p. 321)

5. Interpersonal gains
    Mania and depression have been viewed by some theorists as "social roles." If they are
    roles, what is the goal of the "manic role"? What is the goal of the "depressed role"?   (p. 321)

    Depression has also been viewed as an attempt to communicate. What is the depressed
    person often trying to communicate?   (p. 322)

7. General sociocultural factors
   a. How does the frequency of affective disorders differ in industrialized versus nonindustrialized countries? How does the symptom picture differ? (p. 323)

   b. What type of data suggests that the incidence of depression is related to the degree of stress a person experiences? (pp. 323–324)

8. Treatment and outcomes
   a. Is medication necessary for the treatment of mild depression? (p. 324)

   b. In which cases is treatment with lithium most successful? (p. 324)

   c. Antidepressant drugs are helpful for treatment as well as _____ of affective disorder. (p. 324)

   d. Why would tranquilizers be given to a depressed person? (p. 324)

   e. Why is electroconvulsive therapy often used on patients who present a serious suicide risk? (p. 324)

   f. Is psychotherapy of any help to the depressed person who is already receiving antidepressant drugs, according to Klerman and Schecher (1982)? (p. 324)

g. Describe Beck's (1977) therapeutic approach to depression. (p. 325)

9. Varieties of depression according to DSM-III
   Match the following diagnoses with the appropriate clinical features. (p. 300)

   Diagnosis

   1. major depression

   2. bipolar disorder, depressed

   3. dysthymic disorder

   4. cyclothymic disorder, depressed

   5. adjustment disorder with depressed mood

   Main features

   a. Person is having a major depressive episode; previously had manic episode.

   b. Person has been bothered for two years by a chronic but mild depressed mood.

   c. Person is having a major depressive episode and has had just one previous episode that was also depressive.

   d. Person is depressed after being divorced three months ago.

   e. Person has suffered for the last two years with subclinical episodes of depression.

10. The melancholia subsyndrome
    What is melancholia, and how does it differ from depression? (p. 309)

11. Stressors preceding severe depression
    List the four major stressors found to precede the onset of depression by both Paykel el al. (1973) and Left et al. (1970). (p. 318)

12. Playing the manic game
    Manic people often are disagreeable and threatening to others. Why do they act this way? (p. 322)

13. Suicide
   a. The risk of suicide is significant in depressed persons. The risk of suicide is just _____ percent during the year a depressive episode occurs but rises to _____ percent over the entire lifetime of an individual who experiences recurrent episodes.   (p. 326)
   b. Experts agree that the actual number of suicides is probably _____ times as high as the official number.   (p. 326)
   c. The same factors that are linked to the onset of depression are correlated with suicidal behavior. What are some of these factors?   (p. 328)

   d. Place the following under the headings that properly represent their suicide rate: Australian aborigines, Czechoslovakia, Philippine Islands, United States, Canada, Finland.   (pp. 328–329)

Low Rates	Medium Rates	High Rates
1.	1.	1.
2.	2.	2.

   e. How may religious attitudes influence suicide rates?   (p. 329)

   f. Briefly explain Durkheim's thoughts regarding the relationship of group cohesiveness and suicide.   (p. 330)

   g. What have researchers such as Havighurst (1969) suggested about the relationship between suicide rates and murder rates in a country?   (p. 331)

14. Suicidal ambivalence
   a. Place the following labels on the following diagram to indicate the relative frequency of each type of suicidal person: "to be," "not to be," "to be or not to be."   (p. 331)

1. _____
   (p. 331)

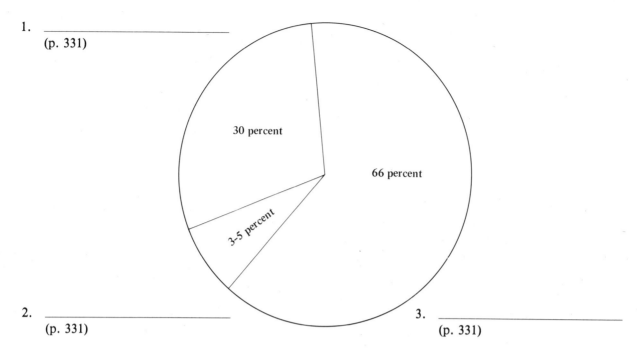

30 percent

66 percent

3-5 percent

2. _____
   (p. 331)

3. _____
   (p. 331)

b. Fill in the missing information in the chart below that summarizes Farberow and Litman's (1970) classification of suicidal behavior. (pp. 331–332)

Group	Feelings About Death	Method of Suicide Selected
1. to be group	Do not wish to die.	
2. not to be group		
3. to be or not to be group		Tend to choose methods that are moderately slow-acting to allow for the possibility of intervention.

15. Communication of suicidal intent
   a. Which of the following is most common: no communication of suicidal intent, direct communication of suicidal intent, or indirect communication of suicidal intent? (p. 332)
   b. Overall, _____ percent of people who successfully committed suicide made a direct or an indirect attempt to communicate their intent. (p. 332)

c. Give common examples of "indirect" communications of suicidal intent.   (p. 332)

16. Suicide notes
    a. Which is more common: a person commits suicide and leaves a note, or a person commits suicide and doesn't leave a note?   (p. 333)

    b. Fill in the missing information on the following chart that summarizes the frequency and content of different types of suicide notes.

Type of Note	Frequency	Content
1. positive emotional content (p. 333)	51 percent	expresses affection, gratitude, concern for others
2. negative emotional content (p. 333)		
3. neutral emotional content (p. 333)		
4. mixed emotional content (p. 333)		

    c. Why does Shneidman (1973) think suicide notes are disappointing?   (pp. 334–335)

17. Suicide prevention
    a. Why don't many suicidal persons voluntarily seek help?   (p. 335)

    b. What is the primary objective of crisis intervention therapy?   (p. 335)

    c. List the five goals that are emphasized in crisis intervention with suicidal persons.   (p. 335)
        1.

        2.

        3.

4.

5.

c. Why is a person who has made a previous suicide attempt at a particularly high risk for suicide? (p. 335)

d. Farberow (1974) states that two types of people come to a suicide prevention center. (pp. 336–337)
   1. Describe the larger group (60–65 percent of persons coming to a suicide prevention center), and indicate the treatment they should receive.

   2. Describe the smaller group (35–40 percent), and indicate the treatment they should receive.

e. What did Sawyer, Sudack, and Hall (1972) find in their study of 53 persons who committed suicide even after contact with a suicide prevention center? (p. 337)

   How has this study influenced the treatment offered in suicide prevention centers? (p. 337)

f. Describe some of the measures that suicide prevention centers can adopt to
   1. focus on high risk groups. (p. 337)

   2. broaden the scope of their programs. (p. 337)

(18.) Ethical issues in suicide prevention
   a. Why do many professionals believe that suicide prevention centers should exist, even though a "right to die" may exist in some cases? (pp. 338–339)

19. Warning signs for student suicide
    a. List some of the signs that indicate a student may be suicidal. (p. 329)

    b. Do students commit suicide because they are doing poorly in school? (p. 329)

    c. Is the breakup of a romance more likely to cause suicide in women than in men? (p. 329)

(20.) How a suicide prevention center answers calls for help
    a. What are the five steps that must be accomplished in counseling a suicidal person? (p. 336)
        1.

        2.

        3.

        4.

        5.

(21.) Lethality scale for assessment of suicide potentiality
    a. Fill in the missing information in the following table that summarizes indicators of greater probability of suicide. (p. 338)

124

Category	Suicide More Probable if:
1. age and sex	Individual is male and individual is over 50.
2. symptoms	
3. stress	
4. acute versus chronic aspects	
5. suicidal plan	
6. resources	
7. prior suicidal behavior	
8. medical status	
9. communication aspects	
10. reaction of significant others	

CHAPTER QUIZ

1. Which of the following is *not* one of the psychological variables involved in normal depression among college students?
    a. sexuality
    b. dependency
    c. inefficacy
    d. self-criticism.
2. A disorder which involves mood swings between subclinical levels of depression and mania is
    a. bipolar disorder.
    b. manic depression.
    c. cyclothymic disorder.
    d. dysthymic disorder.
3. Which of the following is a symptom of depression?
    a. marked expansive mood
    b. outbursts of irritability
    c. unrelievable restlessness
    d. fatigue.

4. Which of the following statements accurately describes an aspect of the clinical course of recurrent affective disorder?
    a. An episode lasts nine months.
    b. Approximately 30 percent of persons experience recurrent episodes.
    c. Between episodes the patient is essentially normal.
    d. Approximately 40 percent of persons experience complete recovery.
5. Compared to persons who suffer from major depression, persons with bipolar affective disorder
    a. experience their first episode at an older age.
    b. suffer more episodes in the course of their lifetimes.
    c. have a lower suicide mortality rate.
    d. have a more favorable full recovery rate.
6. The rate of bipolar affective disorder is _____ percent among close relatives (brothers, sisters, parents) of patients with a bipolar affective disorder compared to _____ percent in the general population.
    a. 30 percent; 1 percent
    b. 15 percent; 0.5 percent
    c. 7 percent; 2 percent
    d. 5 percent; 3 percent.
7. All the following have been suggested as biological causes of bipolar affective disorder *except*
    a. inhibition/excitation imbalance.
    b. X-linked genetic abnormality.
    c. levels of biogenic amines.
    d. acetylcholine depletion.
8. According to Paykel, the most frequent stressor reported to occur just prior to the patient's early symptoms was
    a. death or serious illness of family member.
    b. serious personal illness.
    c. marital difficulties.
    d. changes in work conditions.
9. Learned helplessness refers to the depressed patient's perception that
    a. accustomed reinforcement is no longer forthcoming.
    b. there is no way to cope with the stress.
    c. reinforcement is inadequate.
    d. the world is a negative place.
10. For most psychotic depressive patients the treatment of choice is
    a. lithium carbonate.
    b. imipramine or amitriptyline.
    c. ECT.
    d. cognitively oriented therapy.
11. Which of the following statements regarding men and suicide is accurate?
    a. Three times as many men as women commit suicide.
    b. The most commonly used method is drug ingestion.
    c. The rate of completed suicides is increasing faster among men than women.
    d. Three times as many men as women attempt suicide.
12. Which of the following countries has a relatively low suicide rate?
    a. Norway
    b. Finland

c. Sweden
d. Czechoslovakia

13. Most people who contemplate suicide
    a. are seemingly intent on dying.
    b. are ambivalent about dying.
    c. leave the question of death to chance.
    d. do not wish to die but rather to communicate dramatically.

14. At least 60 percent of the persons who committed suicide that Rudestam (1971) studied had
    a. made direct verbal threats of their intent.
    b. made indirect verbal threats.
    c. left suicide notes.
    d. called a suicide prevention center.

15. Real suicide notes when compared to fake suicide notes contain more
    a. neutral thoughts.
    b. positive content.
    c. negative content.
    d. incomprehensible content.

10

Schizophrenic disorders and paranoia

OVERVIEW

The most severe derangement of human behavior possible may be seen in some of the more severe cases of schizophrenia. Thus, this condition fascinates many people, including psychologists. Because schizophrenia involves disorders in thought, perception, affect, motor behavior, and social relationships, researchers have hoped that study of schizophrenics might lead to a better understanding of how these phenomena operate.

Several different types of schizophrenia are described in Chapter 10 and then the causal factors of the whole group are discussed. There are many different studies described, since the causes of schizophrenia have been more thoroughly researched than many of the other conditions studied so far. Finally, the treatment of schizophrenia—mainly with drugs—is described and evaluated. The chapter concludes with a short discussion of the rather rare clinical syndrome of paranoia.

TERMS YOU SHOULD KNOW

the schizophrenias (p. 344)

dementia praecox (p. 344)

process schizophrenia (p. 349)

reactive schizophrenia (p. 349)

cognitive slippage (pp. 350–351)

breakdown of perceptual selectivity (p. 351)

hallucinations (p. 351)

anhedonia (p. 351)

"blunting" of affect (p. 351)

undifferentiated type (of schizophrenia) (p. 354)

catatonic type (of schizophrenia) (p. 356)

catatonic stupor (p. 356)

echopraxia (p. 357)

echolalia (p. 357)

disorganized (hebephrenic) type (of schizophrenia) (p. 358)

paranoid type (of schizophrenia) (p. 359)

delusions (p. 360)

residual type (of schizophrenia) (p. 362)

residual type (of schizophrenia) (p. 362)

schizoaffective disorder (p. 362)

schizophreniform disorder (p. 362)

twin studies (p. 363)

adoption strategy (p. 363)

family studies (p. 366)

high risk children (p. 367)

endogenous hallucinogen (p. 367)

transmethylation hypothesis (p. 367)

autointoxication (pp. 367–368)

dopamine hypothesis (p. 368)

schizophrenogenic mothers and fathers (p. 373)

marital schism (p. 374)

marital skew (pp. 374–375)

pseudomutuality (p. 375)

double bind (p. 375)

amorphous style (of thinking) (p. 375)

fragmented style (of thinking) (p. 375)

paranoia (p. 387)

acute paranoid disorder (p. 387)

(folie à deux) (p. 388)

paranoid illumination (p. 393)

paranoid pseudocommunity (p. 394)

CONCEPTS TO MASTER

1. Introduction
    a. In what sense are schizophrenia and paranoia the opposite of the affective disorders?   (p. 343)

    b. Why do the authors of the text call schizophrenia the ultimate breakdown?   (p. 343)

    c. Does schizophrenia mean the same thing as multiple personality?   (p. 344)

    d. In the United States the incidence of schizophrenia is _____ percent of the popu-
        lation.   (p. 345)
        Are all of these people actively receiving treatment?   (p. 345)

    e. What is the median age (the age that has exactly half the cases below it and half the cases above
        it) of first admission to a psychiatric hospital with a diagnosis of schizophrenia?   (p. 345)

    f. Give several reasons why schizophrenia is considered the most serious of all psychotic
        disorders.   (p. 345)

2. A case study
    a. Is it possible to make an estimate of how much of the Genain's schizophrenia was due to
        heredity and how much was due to environment?   (p. 349)

3. Clinical picture in schizophrenia
    a. The following diagram represents the process-reactive distribution. Place an *H* where Hester
        Genain would fall on the distribution. (She was the quadruplet who was never as well off as her
        sisters and moved in imperceptible steps toward serious deterioration.) Place an *M* where Myra
        Genain would fall. (She was the least disturbed quadruplet before her breakdown and was able
        to regain effective control of her life afterwards.)   (p. 349)

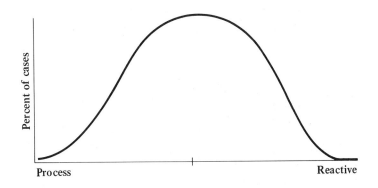

Process   Reactive

b. The DSM–III presents criteria characteristic of the schizophrenic disorders, although all of them would not be seen in every case. These characteristics are listed in the chart on page 132. Fill in the empty boxes by writing a short description of the characteristic or providing a clinical example chosen from the text to illustrate the characteristic as appropriate.

4. Problems in defining schizophrenic behavior
   a. What is the origin of the criteria for schizophrenia presented in DSM–III? (p. 353)

   b. Which set of diagnostic criteria results in the largest number of persons diagnosed as schizophrenic: DSM–II or DSM–III? (p. 353)

   c. Sarbin and Mancuso (1980) state that schizophrenia is a moral verdict. Explain their view. (p. 353)

   d. Bellak (1979) states that schizophrenia is the "common pathway" of severe adaptive break-down. What does he mean? (p. 353)

   e. Indicate whether the following statements are true or false.
      1. All symptoms of schizophrenia occur in every case. True False (p. 354)
      2. There are universally accepted signs of the presence of schizophrenia. True False (p. 354)
      3. The symptom picture in schizophrenia may change over time. True False (p. 354)
      4. Most schizophrenics fade in or out of reality. True False (p. 354)
      5. Acute schizophrenia may clear up rapidly or progress to a chronic condition. True False (p. 354)
   f. What did the study by Rosenhan (1973) demonstrate? (p. 354)

131

Characteristics of Schizophrenia

Characteristic	Brief Description	Clinical Example
1. disorganization of a previous level of functioning (p. 350)	There is impairment in routine areas of daily functioning.	Patient stops taking baths and wearing clean clothes.
2. disturbance of language and communication (p. 350)		Patient says, "I'm growing my father's hair."
3. disturbance in content of thought (p. 351)	Many types of delusions may be seen.	
4. disturbance in perception (p. 351)	Breakdown in perceptual filtering occurs. Hallucinations may be seen.	
5. disturbance in affect (p. 351)	inappropriate affect anhedonia	Patient laughs uproariously upon receipt of news of a parent's death. Patient can't recall the last time he or she was happy.
6. confused sense of self (p. 351)		Patient feels he or she is tied up to universal powers.
7. disturbed volition (p. 351)	A disruption of goal-directed activity occurs.	
8. disturbed relationship with external world (autism) (p. 351)		Young person develops a fantasy world and spends most of the day conversing with imaginary people.
9. disturbed motor behavior (p. 353)		Patient exhibits excited hyperactivity, apparent clumsiness, stupor, rigid posturing, ritualistic mannerisms, and bizarre grimacing.

5. Types of schizophrenia
   a. Match the following types of schizophrenia with the appropriate definition.

   1. undifferentiated type (p. 354)
   2. paranoid type (p. 359)
   3. catatonic type (p. 356)
   4. disorganized type (p. 358)
   5. residual type (p. 355)
   6. schizoaffective disorder (p. 362)
   7. schizophreniform disorder (p. 362)

   a. those persons who are in remission following a schizophrenic episode and show only mild signs of schizophrenia
   b. a form of schizophrenia that occurs at an early age and includes blunting, inappropriate mannerisms, and bizarre behavior
   c. a person in whom symptoms of schizophrenia have existed for six months or less
   d. a person who shows absurd, illogical, changeable delusions and, frequently, hallucinations
   e. a form of schizophrenia in which all the primary indications of schizophrenia are seen in a rapidly changing pattern
   f. a person who shows some schizophrenic signs as well as obvious depression or elation
   g. a type of schizophrenia characterized by alternating periods of extreme excitement and extreme withdrawal

   b. What has happened to the relative frequency of paranoid schizophrenia and undifferentiated schizophrenia over the last several years? (p. 359)

   c. Under what circumstances might a paranoid schizophrenic become violent? (p. 357)

   d. What has happened to the frequency of catatonic schizophrenia during recent years? (p. 356)

   e. Which is the more common form of catatonic behavior—excited or withdrawn? (p. 356)

   f. What is the prognosis for a disorganized schizophrenic? (p. 359)

6. Biological factors in schizophrenia
   a. The authors of the text consider three general categories of biological causes of schizophrenia: heredity, biochemical factors, and neurophysiological factors. Respond to the following questions regarding these causes.

1. Heredity
    a. Twin studies
        What concordance rates were found by Gottesman and Shields (1972), Cohen et al. (1972), and Kringlen (1967)? (p. 363)

        If schizophrenia were exclusively a genetic disorder, what concordance rate for identical twins would be found? (p. 363)

        What are the criticisms of twin studies? (p. 363)

    b. Adoption studies
        What did Heston (1966) do, and what were his major findings? (p. 366)

        What could these findings mean? (p. 366)

        What unusual findings were reported by Benjamin (1976)? (p. 366)

        What criticisms of the adoption method have been offered by Sarbin and Mancuso (1980)? (p. 366)

    c. Family studies
        Describe the results of Rieder's (1973) study of children raised by their own schizophrenic parents. (p. 366)

Kringlen (1978) found that _____ percent of children born to schizophrenic parents develop psychosis as adults, whereas _____ percent develop entirely normally.   (pp. 366–367)

   d. High risk children
      How well have studies of high risk children paid off?   (p. 367)

   e. What is the authors' overall conclusion regarding a genetic basis for schizophrenia?   (p. 367)

2. Biochemical factors
   Match the following columns:

Hypothesis		**Proposed Mechanism**
1. transmethylation hypothesis	(p. 367)	a. deficient regulation
2. dopamine hypothesis	(p. 368)	b. autointoxication by endogenous hallucinogen
3. enkephalin/endorphin hypothesis	(p. 368)	c. autointoxication by natural opiates

Which of the above hypotheses has the most support?   (p. 368)

3. Neurophysiological factors
   Describe some of the deficiencies in normal attention and information processing that have been observed in schizophrenics.   (p. 368)
   Sarbin and Mancuso (1980) argue that such findings are "guaranteed in advance." How is this so?   (pp. 369–370)
   If the deficiencies do exist, what factors might have caused them?   (p. 370)
   b. What overall conclusions do the authors of the text reach regarding the biological causal factors of schizophrenia?

7. Psychosocial factors in schizophrenia
The authors consider five psychosocial causes of schizophrenia: early psychic trauma, pathogenic family interactions, faulty learning, deficient social roles, and stress. Respond to the following questions regarding them.   (p. 370)
   a. Early psychic trauma
      What do the authors of the text conclude regarding the importance of early psychic traumas (child abuse, separations, divorce, death, etc.) as causal factors in schizophrenia?   (p. 371)

Why does Meehl (1978) believe that it may be very difficult to trace schizophrenia to particular life events? (p. 373)

b. Pathogenic family interactions
How have some studies described the mothers of schizophrenics? How have the fathers of schizophrenics been described? (p. 373)

What have several researchers (e.g., Liem, 1974) noted about the impact of schizophrenic children's behavior on their parents? (p. 374)

Roff and Knight (1981) found that the presence of marital schism and skew among parents was predictive of _____. (p. 375)
Under what circumstances is a schizophrenic's thinking most disturbed according to Bannister (1971)? (p. 378)

Singer et al. (1978, 1979) reported that high "communication defiance" between parents was predictive of _____. (p. 378)

8. Treatment and outcomes
a. What is the chance that a schizophrenic patient admitted to a modern mental hospital and given chemotherapy and modern treatment will be discharged in a matter of weeks? (p. 385)

What is the chance he or she will be readmitted during the first year after release? (p. 385)

b. The overall outcome of schizophrenia can be broken down into three groups. What percentage of schizophrenic patients fall into each of these groups? (p. 385)

_____ percent   1. Those patients who recover from the schizophrenia and remain symptom free for five years.

_____ percent   2. Those patients who show partial recovery with some residual symptoms.

_____ percent   3. Those patients who remain largely or totally disabled for their entire life.

    c. Do forms of psychological therapy exist that are useful in the treatment of schizophrenia?   (p. 386)

9. Paranoia
    a. Paranoia is rarely seen in clinics, because these persons do not come for treatment. What types of people in the community are likely to be suffering from paranoia?   (p. 387)

10. Clinical picture of paranoia
    a. Briefly describe the behavior of a person with paranoia.   (p. 387)

    b. Under what circumstances may paranoid individuals become dangerous?   (p. 390)

11. Causal factors in paranoia
    a. Are biological factors thought to be an important cause of paranoia?   (p. 391)

    b. Describe the family background typical of paranoid persons.   (p. 392)

    c. Describe the type of personality traits characteristic of paranoid people.   (p. 392)

12. Treatment and outcomes
    a. Describe a treatment package useful for patients in the early stages of paranoia.   (pp. 394–395)

b. What type of treatment is effective once a paranoid person's delusional system is well established? (p. 395)

13. Regression to primary thought processes in schizophrenia
   a. How does the regression seen in schizophrenia compare to a child's behavior? (p. 350)

   b. What appears to be the purpose of the regression seen in schizophrenia? (p. 350)

14. Conditions associated with favorable outcomes in the treatment of schizophrenia
   a. What type of background factors have been associated with favorable outcomes in schizophrenia? (p. 386)

   b. What did Hawk, Carpenter, and Strauss (1975) find in their comparison of treatment outcomes' of acute (i.e. reactive) schizophrenics with other types of schizophrenics? (p. 386)

15. Folie à deux
   When folie à deux occurs, what is the most frequent relationship between the affected parties? (p. 388)

16. Sequence of events in paranoid mode of thinking
   Place the following stages in the development of paranoid thinking in their proper order: hostility, protective thinking, paranoid illumination, delusions, suspiciousness. (p. 389)
   1. _____   2. _____

   3. _____   4. _____

   5. _____

CHAPTER QUIZ

1. Schizophrenia is primarily a disorder of
   a. mood.
   b. affect.
   c. information processing.
   d. interpersonal relationships.
2. The incidence of schizophrenia in the United States is
   a. 0.5 percent.
   b. 1 percent.
   c. 2 percent.
   d. 5 percent.
3. The median age of onset for schizophrenia is
   a. below 15.
   b. around 30.
   c. over 45.
   d. older in females than males.
4. Hester Genain was never as well off psychologically as her sisters and moved in imperceptible steps toward psychosis. She could be viewed as a _____ schizophrenic.
   a. acute
   b. residual
   c. process
   d. reactive
5. A schizophrenic's statement that he is "growing his father's hair" is an example of
   a. anhedonia.
   b. autism.
   c. echolalia.
   d. cognitive slippage.
6. At least 50 percent of schizophrenics experience _____ during the onset of their disorders.
   a. breakdown in perceptual filtering
   b. oceanic feelings
   c. pecularities in motor behavior
   d. hallucinations
7. Which of the following statements regarding the clinical picture in schizophrenia is *false?*
   a. There are universally accepted signs of schizophrenia.
   b. The symptom picture among schizophrenics may differ markedly from one individual to another.
   c. Most schizophrenic people fade in and out of reality.
   d. The symptom picture among schizophrenics may change greatly over time.
8. The central feature of _____ schizophrenia is pronounced motor symptoms.
   a. undifferentiated
   b. catatonic
   c. disorganized
   d. paranoid
9. Which of the following statements regarding paranoid schizophrenia is *false?*
   a. This type of schizophrenia is on the increase.
   b. Patients show a higher level of prepsychotic adaptive coping.

c. Vivid hallucinations may occur.

d. Delusions of persecution and grandeur are common.

10. Monitoring over time children born to schizophrenic mothers is the research strategy known as
   a. twin studies.
   b. adoption studies.
   c. family studies.
   d. high risk studies.

11. The hypothesis that suggests that schizophrenia is caused by deficient regulation of naturally produced chemicals is the _____ hypothesis.
   a. transmethylation
   b. autointoxication
   c. dopamine
   d. enkephalin

12. The "schizophrenogenic father" has been described as _____ in his relationship to his son.
   a. rejecting, domineering
   b. cold, overprotective
   c. rigid, moralistic about sex
   d. passive, uninvolved

13. "You got all As. I suppose good grades are pretty easy to get nowadays." This is an example of
   a. pseudomutuality.
   b. undermining personal authenticity.
   c. double bind communication.
   d. fragmented thought.

14. The exaggerated use of defense mechanisms such as _____ may predispose a person to develop hallucinations and delusions.
   a. repression
   b. regression
   c. projection
   d. isolation of affect

15. What proportion of schizophrenic patients remain symptom free for five years?
   a. 10 percent
   b. 30 percent
   c. 50 percent
   d. 60 percent.

11

Substance-use and other addictive disorders

OVERVIEW

It has been estimated that a major proportion of America's health problems are due to self-injurious practices such as excessive drinking, smoking, and overeating. These problems are explored in Chapter 11. They are considered forms of addiction, along with drug use and compulsive gambling.

A great deal of background information is presented to help document the extent of the various addictive behaviors and their costs to society. Treatment approaches that have been developed for each specific addiction are then described.

TERMS YOU SHOULD KNOW

substance-induced organic disorder (p. 397)

toxicity (p. 397)

substance-use disorder (p. 397)

substance-use organic disorder (p. 397)

substance abuse (p. 397)

substance dependence (p. 397)

tolerance (p. 397)

withdrawal symptoms (p. 397)

psychoactive (p. 398)

alcoholic (p. 398)

problem drinker (p. 398)

blackouts (p. 402)

hangover (p. 402)

(fetal alcohol syndrome) (p. 403)

spree drinkers (p. 404)

multiple addictions (p. 404)

alcoholic psychoses (p. 404)

pathological intoxication (p. 404)

delirium tremens (p. 405)

acute alcoholic hallucinosis (p. 406)

Korsakoff's psychosis (p. 407)

alcoholic personality (p. 408)

detoxification (p. 412)

disulfuram (Antabuse) (p. 412)

community reinforcement approach (p. 413)

covert sensitization (p. 414)

controlled drinking treatment (p. 414)

behavioral self-control training (p. 414)

Alcoholics Anonymous (AA) (p. 416)

Al-Anon (p. 416)

indulgent behaviors (p. 418)

opium (p. 420)

alkaloids (p. 420)

morphine (p. 420)

analgesic (p. 420)

heroin (p. 420)

codeine (p. 420)

Harrison Act (p. 420)

shorting (p. 421)

skin popping (p. 421)

mainlining (p. 421)

rush (p. 421)

withdrawal symptoms (p. 421)

(cross tolerance) (p. 425)

receptor sites (p. 425)

endorphins (p. 425)

methadone hydrochloride (p. 427)

barbiturates (p. 427)

silent abusers (p. 428)

potentiates (p. 428)

amphetamines (p. 429)

schedule II substances (p. 430)

narcolepsy (p. 430)

amphetamine psychosis (p. 430)

cocaine (p. 431)

hallucinogens (p. 432)

humanity identification (p. 433)

bad trip (pp. 433–434)

flashbacks (p. 434)

marijuana (p. 435)

hashish (p. 435)

reverse tolerance (p. 436)

a-motivational syndrome (p. 438)

hyperobesity (p. 438)

adipose cells (p. 439)

developmental obesity (p. 439)

reactive obesity (p. 439)

externality hypothesis (p. 439)

TOPS (p. 441)

anorexigenic drugs (p. 442)

jejunoileal bypass operation (p. 442)

pathological gambling (p. 442)

CONCEPTS TO MASTER

1. Introduction
   a. Fill in the missing blanks in the following schematic representation of the DSM–III classification of substance related disorders. (p. 397)

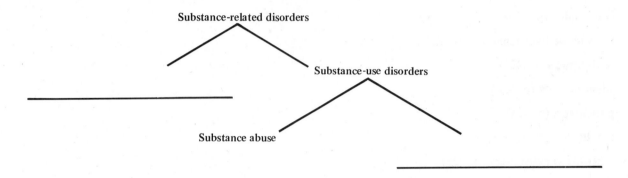

Substance-related disorders

Substance-use disorders

Substance abuse

2. Incidence and effects of problem drinking
   a. Alcoholism has varying definitions. The World Health Organization has a very broad definition that would include many people. Behaviorists conceptualize alcoholism as the very extreme point on the continuum of problem drinking. The authors of the text adopt the definition of the President's Commission on Mental Health. How does this group define alcoholism? (p. 398)

   b. Approximately _____ million Americans experience abusive use of alcohol, but only about _____ million receive treatment. (p. 399)
   c. List some of the ways alcoholism is a drain on society. (p. 399)

   d. What is the ratio of male alcoholics to female alcoholics? (p. 399)

3. Clinical picture of alcohol abuse and dependence
   a. Why has alcohol been called a catalyst for violence? (p. 400)

144

b. How much alcohol do you have to have in your body to be considered intoxicated? (p. 400)

c. What organ of the body works on assimilating the alcohol into the system? (p. 402)

d. How can excessive intake of alcohol lead to malnutrition? (p. 402)

e. Jellinek (1952 and 1971) studied 2,000 drinkers and described four common stages through which they progress. Fill in the missing information on the following chart that summarizes the characteristics of each of the stages.

Stage of Alcohol Dependence	Characteristics
1. prealcoholic symptomatic phase (p. 403)	a. How did alcoholics drink when they first started? b. What did alcohol do more strongly for them than it does for regular social drinkers?

2. prodromal phase (p. 403)	a. This second phase is marked by some serious signals such as _____.
	b. Certain special signs of alcoholism appear in this phase, including
	  1. secret drinking to avoid criticism
	  2. _____
	  3. _____
	  4. _____.

3. crucial phase (p. 403)	a. In this phase any consumption of alcohol begins a chain reaction that only stops when _____. b. Defense behavior becomes marked, including rationalization and compensation. Give an example that illustrates each defensive maneuver. c. Serious physical problems arise, including _____.
4. chronic phase (p. 403)	a. Loss of tolerance is seen. What is this? What causes it?

f. List two criticisms of Jellinek's phases of alcohol dependence.   (pp. 403–404)

g. Delirium tremens (D.T.s) is a form of psychosis that may occur following a long drinking bout or a physical disease or injury. Also, it may occur upon sudden withdrawal from alcohol. Describe the type of symptoms that are seen in D.T.s. How long do these symptoms usually last?   (p. 405)

h. Currently, is acute alcoholic hallucinosis attributed solely to the effect of alcohol?   (p. 406)

i. Describe the memory deficit that occurs in Korsakoff's psychosis. What is thought to be its cause?   (p. 407)

4. Causes of alcohol abuse and dependence
    a. Biological factors
        Some investigators have questioned whether some people are predisposed to become alcoholic by inherited unusual cravings for alcohol or tendencies toward loss of control. Relevant research includes the following studies. Describe what was done and what was found in each of them.   (pp. 407–408)
        1. Winokur et al. (1970)

        2. Roe, Burks, Mittlemann (1945)

        3. Goodwin et al. (1973)

4. Goodwin et al. (1974)

What overall conclusions do the authors of the text reach on the basis of these data? (p. 408)

At this point in time, is there any conclusive evidence that certain ethnic groups have abnormal physiological reactions to alcohol? (p. 408)

b. Psychosocial factors

The authors suggest that three psychosocial factors contribute to alcoholism: alcoholic personality, stress/reinforcement, and marital relationships. Respond to the following questions regarding these factors.

1. Alcoholic Personality

What do the authors of the text mean by the expression *an alcoholic personality*? (p. 408)

Why is it difficult to determine if an alcoholic personality exists from interviews with people who are alcoholics? (p. 409)

What results have been obtained in prospective studies, such as Loper et al. (1973)? (p. 409)
How did Loper et al. obtain their data? (p. 409)

What are the general personality characteristics of alcoholics once their drinking has become well established? (p. 409)

2. Stress/reinforcement
Schaefer (1971) has concluded that alcoholism is a conditioned response to anxiety. Describe how such a conditioned response would be maintained. (p. 409)

Some critics respond that alcoholism could not possibly be a conditioned response, since its consequences are so negative (e.g. passing out, vomiting, hangover, arguments with spouse and employer, etc.) How does Bandura (1969) respond to these arguments? (p. 409)

3. Marital relationships
How can an alcoholic parent's behavior serve as a model that results in some children in the family becoming alcoholics and others becoming highly negative about the use of alcohol? (p. 410)

Are there any special times of life when alcoholism is apt to begin? (p. 410)

How important is alcoholism as a cause of marital discord? (p. 410)

c. Sociocultural factors
Bales (1946) described three cultural factors that determined whether a specific group would have a high or low rate of alcoholism. What were these factors? (p. 411)
1.

2.

3.

Alcoholism is a major problem among Eskimos in rural Alaska. Why does the United States Public Health Service believe this is so? (p. 411)

Place the following groups and countries under the heading that accurately represents their rate of alcoholism: United States, Moslem countries, France, Jews, Soviet Union, Mormons. (p. 411)

High Rates of Alcoholism   **Exceedingly Low Rates of Alcoholism**

Thus it appears that religious sanctions and social customs can determine whether
_____. (p. 412)

5. Treatment and outcomes
   a. A _____ approach to the treatment of drinking problems appear to be most effective. _____
   treatment appears to be as effective as inpatient treatment. The objectives of treatment programs include physical rehabilitation, _____, and
   _____. (p. 412)
   b. Why are drugs such as chlordiazepoxide (librium, a minor tranquilizer) used during the detoxification process?

   Why might a drug such as disulfuram (Antabuse) be used? (p. 412)

   Antabuse is not considered a complete treatment for alcoholism. Why not?

   c. Sometimes spouses and children of alcoholics are included in group therapy. List three reasons this is done. (p. 413)
      1.

      2.

      3.

d. There are several behavior approaches to treating alcoholism. One involves injecting an emetic (i.e. a drug that causes the person to become extremely nauseated and to vomit). What does the patient do after receiving the injection? (p. 413)

e. Emetic drugs and shock are not always used. Covert sensitization can be used instead. Describe this treatment. (p. 414)

f. Sobell and Sobell (1973) videotaped intoxicated alcoholics. Why did they do this? (p. 414) Then "behavior change" sessions were conducted. What happened in them? Why is the Sobell's research controversial? (p. 414)

g. Several other approaches exist to teaching controlled drinking (Miller and Munoz, 1976; Lovibond and Cady, 1970). How does this approach work? Is it accepted as effective? (pp. 414–415)

h. What is the position of AA on controlled drinking? (p. 416)

i. Briefly describe how AA and Al-Anon family groups operate. (p. 416)

j. Brandsma et al. (1980) suggested that AA had a high dropout rate. Why?

k. Polich et al. (1981) studied the course of alcoholism after treatment. Fill in the percentages they reported among treated alcoholics with serious drinking: (pp. 416–417)

       _____ percent abstained for 4 years,

       _____ percent showed alcohol-related problems,

       _____ percent maintained alcohol dependency, and

       _____ percent had alcohol-related adverse consequences.

l.   Under what conditions is treatment for alcoholism likely to be most effective?   (p. 417)

m.   Describe the cognitive-behavioral approach to relapse prevention.   (p. 418)

6.   Opium and its derivatives (narcotics)

    a.   How is heroin made from morphine?

        What did chemists originally think they were going to accomplish through this procedure?   (p. 420)

    b.   What has happened to the rate of heroin addiction during the 1970s?   (p. 421)

7.   Effects of morphine and heroin

    a.   What happens if a person takes heroin repeatedly for 30 days?   (p. 421)

        What is likely to happen if this person now stops taking the heroin abruptly?   (p. 421)

        Is withdrawal from heroin dangerous and painful?   (p. 421)

    b.   What are the effects of heroin use during pregnancy?   (p. 424)

8. Causal factors in opiate abuse and dependence
   a. What is the single most common cause for heroin use given by addicts?   (pp. 424–425)

   b. The authors present four causes for opiate addiction: physiological causes, relief of pain, psychopathology, and association with a drug subculture. Respond to the following questions regarding these causes.
   Physiological causes
   There are two different types of receptor sites for narcotic drugs. What are they?   (p. 425)
   1.

   2.

   Explain the possible role of endorphins in drug addiction.   (p. 425)

   Relief of pain

   Do the authors place much value on an addict's statement that he/she became addicted to drugs during an illness?   (p. 426)

   Psychopathology
   What type of personality disorder has been found in a large number of addicts studied by Gilbert and Lombardi (1967)?   (p. 426)

   Summarize Chinlund's (1969) characterization of the female addict.   (p. 426)

   Drug subculture
   What changes are seen in the young addict who has joined the drug subculture?   (p. 426)

9. Treatment and outcomes
   a. How successful were English hospitals at curing addiction with group and individual counseling?   (p. 427)

b. Describe the research that Dole et al. (1968, 1969) did with methadone hydrochloride.   (p. 427)

    Why hasn't this treatment been as successful when applied generally as it was in the research studies?   (p. 427)

c. List the pros and cons of methadone maintenance programs:

    Pros   **Cons**

10. The barbiturates (sedatives)
     a. What age group is most often found to be addicted to barbiturates?   (p. 428)

     b. How can barbiturates cause death?   (p. 428)

     c. What happens after prolonged, excessive use of barbiturates?   (p. 428)

11. Causal factors in barbiturate abuse and dependence
     a. Who typically becomes dependent on barbiturates?   (p. 428)

     b. What type of personality problems might lead a person to seek relief from barbiturates?   (p. 428)

12. Treatment and outcomes
     a. Describe the typical symptoms of barbiturate withdrawal.   (p. 428)

     b. How can these symptoms be minimized?   (p. 428)

13. The amphetamines and cocaine (stimulants)
    a. What are the legitimate medical uses of amphetamines? (p. 430)

    b. Are amphetamines addicting? (p. 430)

       Does one build up tolerance to them? (p. 430)

    c. What are the major physiological effects of taking amphetamines? (p. 430)

    d. When does amphetamine psychosis occur? (p. 430)

       How can this condition lead to acts of violence? (p. 430)

    e. What happens when an established user of amphetamines abruptly stops taking the drug? (pp. 430–431)

    f. What are the effects of taking cocaine? (p. 431)

       What is the "cocaine bug"? (p. 431)

14. LSD and related drugs (hallucinogens)
    a. Name four hallucinogenic drugs. (p. 432)
       1.

154

2.

3.

4.

    b.   What effects does LSD have on sensory perception?   (p. 433)

        What is "humanity identification"?   (p. 433)

    c.   Under what circumstances is LSD likely to lead to a bad, as opposed to a good, trip according to the research of Blacker (1968)?   (p. 434)

    d.   Can LSD induce psychosis in a person who only takes the drug once and who has previously been well adjusted?   (p. 434)

    e.   Is there evidence that LSD enhances creativity?   (p. 434)

    f.   How difficult is it to treat dependence on LSD?   (p. 434)

15.   Marijuana
    a.   What is the difference between marijuana and hashish?   (p. 435)

    b.   During the 1970s what proportion of teenagers and young adults experimented with marijuana?   (p. 435)

    c.   Describe the physical effects of marijuana.   (p. 436)
        Psychological effects: pleasurable experiences seem to be enhanced but use may lead to unpleasant feelings if the drug is taken when unhappy or angry.   (p. 436)
        Short-range physiological effects: _____ (p. 436)

d. How likely is marijuana to cause problems for which one has to be hospitalized as compared to alcohol and barbiturates? (p. 436)

e. Does marijuana lead to dependence? (p. 436)

Does a person build up a tolerance to marijuana? (p. 436)

f. Respond true or false to the following controversial statements regarding marijuana.

There are important personality differences between users and nonusers.	True	False	(p. 437)
Marijuana has some adverse effects on physical health.	True	False	(p. 437)
Marijuana has beneficial medical uses.	True	False	(p. 437)
Marijuana enhances creativity.	True	False	(pp. 437–438)

g. What are the arguments against legalization of marijuana use? (p. 438)

16. Extreme obesity
    a. The population of the United States is 220 million. How many of these people are overweight according to Jeffrey and Katz (1977)? (p. 438)

    b. How does obesity put a person at greater risk for death? (p. 438)

17. Causes of persistent overeating
    a. How can overfeeding a child predispose him or her to obesity in adulthood? (p. 439)

    b. Is there any research support for the view that obesity is a response to parental rejection? (p. 439)

c. What is the behavioral explanation of obesity?   (p. 440)

d. Obesity is more common among lower-class people. Why is this?   (p. 441)

18. Treatment of extreme obesity
    a. What is the average outcome of diets according to Stuart (1967)?   (p. 441)

    b. What type of treatment has been found to be most effective for obesity?   (p. 441)

    c. What do the authors of the text conclude about the effectiveness of the following methods
        of losing weight?   (pp. 441–442)
        1. TOPS and Weight Watchers
        2. fasting or starvation diets
        3. anorexigenic drugs
        4. bypass operations
        5. behavioral management methods

19. Pathological gambling
    a. In what ways can gambling be considered an addictive disorder?   (p. 443)

20. Causal factors in pathological gambling
    a. How can compulsive gambling be explained in learning terms?   (p. 443)

b.   What type of personality factors characterize the compulsive gambler?   (p. 444)

21. Treatment and outcomes
    a.   If a gambler joins a Gambler's Anonymous group, how likely is it that he/she will overcome the
        addiction to gambling?   (p. 445)

    b.   List the treatment approaches used to assist compulsive gamblers at the Brecksville, Ohio,
        Veteran's Administration Medical Center.   (pp. 445–446)

(22.) Fetal alcohol syndrome
       How commonly are birth defects related to alcohol abuse?   (p. 403)

(23.) Alcoholics reporting symptoms of alcohol dependence
       What were the two most frequently reported symptoms?   (p. 405)

(24.) Alcoholism treatment programs in business and industry
       What proportion of the problems brought in by employees are alcohol-related?   (p. 419)

CHAPTER QUIZ

1.   The term currently used to signify psychological and physiological reliance on a particular drug is
    a.   *substance dependence.*
    b.   *substance addiction.*
    c.   *substance abuse.*
    d.   *substance reliance.*
2.   When the police discovered Julian, the alcohol content in his bloodstream was near 0.95 percent.
    Their report probably described Julian as

a. uncoordinated and confused.
b. passed out into unconsciousness.
c. an alcoholic.
d. dead.

3. The _____ stage in alcohol dependence is characterized by the sudden onset of blackouts.
a. prealcoholics symptomatic
b. crucial
c. chronic
d. prodromal

4. Delirium tremens is characterized by
a. mild depression, tremors, and blackouts.
b. hallucinations, acute fear, and disorientation.
c. acute fear, blackouts, and psychotic aggression.
d. neuroses, tremors, and auditory hallucinations.

5. _____ refers to an acute psychotic reaction to alcohol characterized by confusion and disorientation and generally occurs in persons having a low tolerance to the drug.
a. Pathological intoxication
b. Delirium tremens
c. Alcoholic hallucinosis
d. Korsakoff's psychosis

6. The withdrawal symptoms experienced by alcoholics trying to stop long-term drinking patterns indicate that
a. cellular metabolism has adapted to the presence of alcohol in the bloodstream.
b. the individual's reinforced drinking behaviors are undergoig negative reinforcement.
c. extensive cellular and metabolic damage is occurring during the withdrawal process.
d. the alcoholic is experiencing the effects of a need-reduction syndrome.

7. Studies of the family background of alcoholics emphasize risks of becoming alcoholic for persons
a. from broken homes.
b. who were denied open love and affection.
c. with an alcoholic parent.
d. with no religious training or affiliation.

8. The only personality characteristic that appears common to the backgrounds of most problem drinkers is
a. general depression.
b. emotional immaturity.
c. inadequate sexual adjustment.
d. personal maladjustment.

9. A cultural attitude of approbation and permissiveness toward drinking, such as exists in France, generally
a. is correlated with a low rate of alcoholism and problem drinking.
b. is a sign that alcoholism has been accepted as a normal behavior pattern.
c. is associated with the common use of alcohol as a means of coping with stress.
d. has no significant effect on either alcoholism or drinking behavior.

10. Extinction of drinking behavior by associating it with noxious mental images is a procedure called
a. Antabuse.
b. systematic desensitization.

c. covert sensitization.

d. implosive therapy.

11. Controversy has developed regarding the validity of the _____ approach to the treatment of alcoholism.

    a. AA

    b. controlled drinking

    c. total abstinence

    d. Al-Anon

12. In their four year follow-up of a large group of treated alcoholics, Polich et al. (1981) found that _____ percent continued to show alcohol-related problems.

    a. 7

    b. 18

    c. 36

    d. 54

13. Withdrawal from amphetamines usually

    a. is physiologically harmful unless done gradually.

    b. causes hallucinations and a condition known as *amphetamine psychosis.*

    c. causes depression.

    d. is painless, both physically and emotionally.

14. Which of the following statements regarding the role of psychopathology in opiate addiction is false?

    a. Many addicts show psychopathic personality characteristics.

    b. Psychopathology exhibited by addicts may stem from drug addiction.

    c. Addicts are highly impulsive.

    d. Female addicts attempt to gain control through drug usage.

15. Apparently, adipose cells (fat cells)

    a. increase in number and size when an adult gains weight.

    b. have no relation to obesity.

    c. decrease in size, but not number, when an adult loses weight.

    d. change chemical structure in obese adults.

12

Psychosexual disorders and variants

OVERVIEW

   Chapter 12 contains three separate sections that are related to sexual behavior. The first section concerns the sexual dysfunctions. These are problems that may interfere with an individual's full enjoyment of sexual relations. The sexual dysfunctions are not mental disorders. They are simply behaviors that can be changed. The diagnostic label *sexual dysfunction* or *sexual variant* really doesn't tell anything about the personality characteristics of the individual. It describes one aspect of that individual's behavior. These conditions may be seen in any kind of individual—normal or abnormal. The second section discusses behaviors that are considered "sex crimes." Most of these behaviors, such as pedophilia or voyeurism, are considered to be mental disorders.

   The last section discusses homosexuality. Homosexuality is not a mental disorder. It is simply an alternative sexual preference.

TERMS YOU SHOULD KNOW

psychosexual dysfunction (p. 450)

erectile insufficiency (p. 451)

primary insufficiency (p. 451)

secondary insufficiency (p. 451)

premature ejaculation (p. 451)

retarded ejaculation (p. 451)

arousal insufficiency (p. 452)

orgasmic dysfunction (p. 452)

vaginismus (p. 452)

dyspareunia (p. 452)

inhibited sexual desire (p. 452)

sexual moron (p. 454)

(sensate focus) (p. 456)

variant sexual behavior (p. 457)

victimless sexual variants (p. 457)

gender identity disorder (transsexualism) (p. 458)

paraphilia (p. 460)

transvestism (p. 460)

fetishism (p. 462)

voyeurism (p. 464)

exhibitionism (p. 464)

sadism (p. 466)

pathological sadists (p. 467)

masochism (p. 468)

pedophilia (p. 469)

incest (p. 471)

rape (p. 474)

statutory rape (p. 474)

forcible rape (p. 474)

criminal sexual conduct (p. 476)

homosexuality (p. 477)

ego-dystonic homosexuality (p. 477)

lesbianism (p. 479)

(AIDS) (p. 482)

CONCEPTS TO MASTER

1. Dysfunctions affecting the male
   a. Explain the distinction between "primary" and "secondary" erectile insufficiency. (p. 451)

Should men expect to develop erectile insufficiency as they become older?   (p. 451)

b. How often is erectile insufficiency organic? How can insufficiency due to organic causes be differentiated from psychogenic insufficiency?   (p. 451)

c. What is LoPicolo's (1978) rule for determining when a male is a premature ejaculator?   (p. 451)

d. Are men who have retarded ejaculation able to achieve orgasm by any method of stimulation?   (p. 452)

2. Dysfunctions affecting the female
    a. What is the difference between a woman with "arousal insufficiency" and one with "orgasmic dysfunction"?   (p. 452)

    b. Which female dysfunction is most likely to have an organic basis?   (p. 452)

3. Causal factors in sexual dysfunction
    a. The authors consider four causes of sexual dysfunction: faulty learning, feelings of fear, inter-personal problems, and social roles. Respond to the following questions regarding each causal factor.
        1. Faulty learning
            What two ideas may be part of a woman's early training about sex that subsequently exert a negative influence on her ability to fully enjoy sexual relations?   (p. 453)
            1.

            2.

            What may be the result of a young man having his first sexual experience under conditions where he is hurried and fears discovery?   (p. 453)

        2. Feelings of fear
            Cooper (1969) reported that anxiety was a primary problem in _____ percent of men with erectile difficulties.   (p. 454)

Masters and Johnson (1975) have concluded that most sexual dysfunctions in males and females are due to fear and anxiety. This anxiety is based on misinformation in early sex training and later aversive experiences with actual sexual relations. An anxious person often adopts a _____ role during sex that leads him or her to become an observer of the sexual relations rather than a wholehearted participant. In this role the person often worries about the adequacy of his or her performance, and these anxieties serve as distractions and make the sexual performance even worse. (p. 454)

3. Interpersonal problems
   Many investigators believe that an individual should be able to experience pleasure and orgasm with any "personally acceptable partner." However, some couples experience changes in their relationship that lead to a termination of their "acceptability" to each other. What are several situations that can lead to a lack of emotional closeness and a lack of "acceptability" as sexual partners. (p. 454)

4. Social roles
   How do the authors of the text believe that changes in the social roles of women have affected men's sexuality? How have these changes affected women's sexuality? (pp. 454–455)

4. Treatment and outcomes
   a. Masters and Johnson's approach to treating sexual dysfunction combines elements of traditional and behavior therapy and emphasizes direct intervention aimed at
      _____. (p. 455)
   b. After Masters and Johnson's pioneering book, many approaches to treating sexual dysfunction were developed. Most approaches are in general agreement that the following goals are important:
      _____ (p. 455)
   c. What do clinicians mean when they say that a particular sexual dysfunction (such as orgasmic dysfunction) is a "disorder of relationship?" (p. 455)

   d. What range of successful outcomes has been reported by sex therapists? (pp. 455–456)

e. Place the following sexual dysfunctions in the appropriate column to indicate how well they respond to treatment: erectile insufficiency, premature ejaculation, vaginismus, and orgasmic dysfunction. (p. 457)

High Success Rates **Lower Success Rates**

5. Psychosexual variants and deviations
    a. Treatment programs for sexual variants cannot focus solely on removing the deviant sexual behavior. According to writers such as Barlow (1974) and Adams and Sturgis (1977), in addition to techniques to stop the deviant sexuality, three other areas should receive attention in the treatment program. They are: (pp. 457–458)
        1.

        2.

        3.

6. Gender identity: problems and disorder
    a. How important is learning in determining whether a person adopts a male or female social role? (p. 458)

    b. The most functional men and women in our society are androgynous. What does this statement mean? (p. 458)

    c. Gender identity disorder involves profound rejection of one's anatomical sex. How common is it? (pp. 458–459)

    d. Describe the psychosocial factors that Green (1974) found to be common in the backgrounds of transsexual boys. (p. 459)

e. Has behavior therapy or psychotherapy been successful in altering gender identity? (p. 460)

f. Describe what procedures are involved in the following surgical changes of sex: (p. 460)
1. male-to-female

2. female-to-male.

g. What do follow-up studies of persons who have had sex-change surgery indicate about the success and appropriateness of this procedure for some people? (p. 460)

h. Why is it recommended that a person seeking sex-change therapy spend a period of time cross-dressing and taking hormones? (p. 460)

7. The paraphilias
a. How is the paraphiliac who peeps into women's windows distinguished from the man who goes to lunchtime lingerie shows in businessmen's restaurants? (p. 460)

b. Transvestism
Do transvestites see themselves as homosexuals? (p. 460)

How do the personality characteristics of transvestite men compare to those of normal men? (p. 461)

How do the authors of the text explain the cause of transvestism?   (p. 462)

c. Fetishism
    What is most arousing to the fetishist, the fetish or the illegal act of obtaining the
    object?   (p. 463)

    How can fetishes be developed through conditioning?   (p. 463)

d. Voyeurism
    What age group commits the majority of voyeuristic acts?   (p. 464)

    What type of person is most likely to be drawn to voyeurism?   (p. 464)

    If a voyeur is married, how well adjusted would he be expected to be in his sexual rela-
    tionships with his wife?   (p. 464)

    Why doesn't pornography seem to satisfy most voyeurs?   (p. 464)

e. Exhibitionism
    How common is exhibitionism in the following countries?   (p. 464)
    1. United States

    2. Europe

    3. Japan

Witzig (1968) studies exhibitionists. He reported that approximately 60 percent of them were
immature. What else did he find about them in the following areas?

1. sexual knowledge (p. 465)

2. attitudes toward masturbation (p. 465)

3. sexual adjustment (if married) (p. 465)

4. sense of confidence in masculinity (pp. 465–466)

In what types of mentally disordered people may exhibitionism be seen, in addition to the inadequate, immature persons described above? (p. 466)

Exhibitionism may also be related to life stress. During periods of stress an individual may regress to adolescent _____ and exhibit himself. (p. 466)

f. Sadism
What is a "pathological sadist"? (p. 467)

What are the three causal factors of sadism mentioned by the authors of the text? (p. 468)

g. Masochism
How do patterns of masochistic behavior usually develop? (pp. 468–469)

What does it mean to say that sadism and masochism require a "shared complementary interpersonal relationship"? (p. 469)

h. Pedophilia

In pedophilia the sex object is a _____ and the intimacy usually involves
_____. (p. 469)

The average age of pedophiliacs is _____ years old. By a ratio of 2 to 1,
_____ are most often victimized. (p. 469)

Respond to the following questions.

1. Are most pedophiliacs known to their victims?   Yes   No   (p. 469)
2. Do most pedophiliacs use force?   Yes   No   (p. 469)
3. Is pedophilia usually a one-time event?   Yes   No   (p. 469)
4. Does the victim of a pedophiliac actively participate?   Yes   No   (p. 469)

Briefly describe each of the following types of offenders:

1. the immature offender (p. 470)

2. the regressed offender (p. 470)

3. the conditioned offender (p. 470)

4. the psychopathic offender. (p. 470)

8. Other psychosexual deviations

a. Incest

Describe the consequences of inbreeding. (pp. 471–472)

Incest is thought to be grossly underreported to authorities, but Meiselman (1978) estimates
the incidence at 1–2 per _____ persons. (p. 472)
What is the most common form of incest? (p. 472)

How common is mother-son incest compared to father-daughter? (p. 472)

What is "situational incest"? (p. 472)

What forms of psychopathology may be related to incest? (p. 472)

What impact does an incestuous relationship between father and daughter have on the sons of the family if they become aware of it? (p. 472)

Is incest likely to occur in a home where the parents have a good marital relationship? (p. 472)

Describe the fathers studied by Cavillin (1966) who came to the attention of police authorities in the following areas: (pp. 472–473)
1. history of mental disorder (p. 472)

2. history of extramarital affairs (p. 472)

3. average age of father (p. 473)

4. average age of daughter (p. 473)

5. father's feelings toward the mother. (p. 473)

6. Describe the feelings of the abused daughter. (p. 473)

b. Rape
    What has happened to the incidence of rape over the last ten years?   (p. 474)

    Why do four out of five rape victims fail to report their rape to the police?   (p. 474)

    How old is the typical rapist?   (p. 474)

    Respond to the following questions by circling the appropriate answer: (p. 474)
    1. Rape is a young man's crime.   Yes No
    2. Rape is a repetitive activity.   Yes No
    3. Most rapes are planned.   Yes No
    4. A third of rapes involve more than one offender.   Yes No
    5. The closer the relationship between victim and offender, the more brutally the victim
        may be beaten.   Yes No
    Describe the characterization of the woman repeatedly victimized by rape found by Calhoun
    et al. (1982).   (p. 475)

    Although rape involves sexual relations, did Groth et al. (1977) discover a single case where
    sexual satisfaction was the rapist's primary motive?   (p. 475)

    Briefly describe the following types of rapists:
    1. power-assertive   (p. 475)

    2. power reassurance   (p. 475)

    3. anger-retaliation   (p. 475)

4.   anger-excitation.   (p. 475)

Label the following diagram to illustrate how frequently each of these types of rapist occur: (p. 475)

1. _____

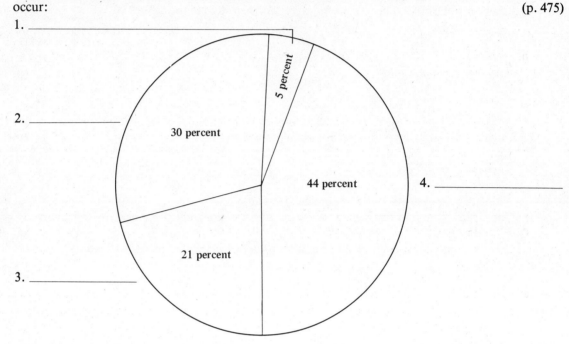

2. _____

30 percent

5 percent

44 percent   4. _____

21 percent

3. _____

9. Treatment and outcomes
    a. Most sexually variant acts cannot be adequately conceptualized simply as aberrations of sexual arousal. In most instances we also need to look at   (p. 476)
        1.

        2.

        3.

    b. How did Barlow and Abel (1976) (a) modify feminine gender role, (b) improve social skills, (c) increase arousal to heterosexual stimuli and (d) decrease arousal to homosexual stimuli in their treatment of a 17-year-old transsexual male?   (p. 476)

10. Male and female homosexuality
    a. When is homosexuality a mental disorder and when isn't it considered a mental disorder according to the DSM–III? (p. 477)

    b. Kinsey (1948) surveyed the sexual behavior of white male subjects. How frequent were the following experiences? (P. 479)
       _____ percent 1. Homosexual experience to the point of orgasm at least once during adolescence.
       _____ percent 2. As many homosexual encounters as heterosexual.
       _____ percent 3. Exclusively homosexual experience since adolescence.
    c. How do the homosexual experiences reported by women differ from those reported by men? (p. 479)

    d. What have laboratory studies of arousal revealed about bisexuality? (pp. 480–481)

    e. The authors consider five causal factors of homosexuality: genetic and hormonal factors, positive reinforcement of homosexual experiences, negative conditioning of heterosexual experiences, family patterns, and sociocultural factors. Respond to the following questions about each causal factor.
       1. Genetic and hormonal factors
          Kallman reported a _____ percent concordance rate for homosexuality among identical twins. Money and his associates have looked at male hormone levels during _____ to understand homosexuality. (p. 481)
       2. Early homosexual experiences
          Early homosexual experiences are reported as pleasurable but under what circumstances do they lead to adult homosexuality? (p. 483)

       3. Negative heterosexual experiences
          What circumstances could lead to the negative conditioning of heterosexual behavior? (p. 483)

4. Family patterns
Describe the common family background Bieber et al. (1962) found among male homosexuals. (pp. 483–485)

Although these findings have been repeated a number of times, they have also been challenged. How do the authors conclude that family background is related to homosexuality? (p. 485)

5. General socoicultural patterns
Under what circumstances might the rate of homosexuality rise in a society? (p. 485)

11. Treatment of sexual dysfunction
   a. Masters and Johnson (1970) have estimated that _____ percent of American marriages suffer from sexual inadequacy, and they consider this fact partially responsible for the high divorce rate. (p. 456)
   b. Masters and Johnson view sexual inadequacy as a form of faulty _____ which probably extend(s) to other areas of the couple's relationship as well. (p. 456)
   c. Briefly describe the three basic components of Masters and Johnson's approach. (p. 456)
      1.

      2.

      3.

   d. In only _____ percent of cases was treatment of sexual dysfunction unsuccessful. (p. 456)

12. Sexual molestation of young children
   a. Why don't professionals recognize even blatant cases of abuse? (p. 473)

174

b.　Who is most frequently the offender in child molestation cases?　(p. 473)

(13.) Should homosexuality be treated?
There are experts who argue that homosexuality should be treated and experts who argue that it should not be treated. Briefly present the views of both sides.
1.　Psychologists should offer treatment to homosexuals because:　(p. 479)

2.　Psychologists should not offer treatment to homosexuals because:　(p. 479)

(14.) AIDS: The gay plague
How is AIDS transmitted?　(p. 482)

(15.) The Masters and Johnson (1979) perspective on homosexuality
a.　Describe the sample studied by Masters and Johnson.　(p. 480)

b.　In what senses may this sample be unrepresentative of homosexuals in general?　(p. 480)

c.　How did Masters and Johnson find homosexuals and heterosexuals compared in the following areas?　(p. 480)
1.　sexual efficiency

2.　fantasies males have

3.　fantasies females have

4. communication regarding sexual preferences and needs

5. patterns of lovemaking

d. How successful were Masters and Johnson in achieving "reorientation" among the homosexuals who came to them for treatment?   (p. 480)

CHAPTER QUIZ

1. Mark, who is the father of two children, has become unable to maintain an erection long enough to complete intravaginal ejaculation. His dysfunction is known as
    a. primary impotence.
    b. secondary erectile insufficiency.
    c. tertiary prematurity.
    d. ejaculatory incompetence.
2. LoPiccolo (1978) has suggested that the male who is unable to tolerate _____ of genital stimulation without ejaculation is probably a candidate for sex therapy.
    a. four minutes
    b. ten minutes
    c. 16 minutes
    d. 22 minutes
3. Janice is 24 years old, married, and apparently well-adjusted in most aspects of her life. She is unable, however, to achieve orgasm. According to the research of Masters and Johnson (1970), Janice's difficulty is probably related to
    a. a conditioned notion that her primary responsibility is to satisfy her husband.
    b. interpersonal difficulties in her marriage.
    c. a hormonal imbalance.
    d. a conditioned fear that sexual intercourse is painful.
4. Success rates approaching 100 percent have been reported with competent sex therapy for
    a. erectile insufficiency.
    b. secondary impotence.
    c. primary orgasmic dysfunction.
    d. premature ejaculation.
5. An example of victimless sexual variants is
    a. voyeurism.
    b. exhibitionism.
    c. sadism.
    d. transvestism.

6. An adult whose background was characterized by encouragement of feminine behavior, maternal overprotection, and lack of male friends would most likely receive which diagnosis?
   a. homosexuality
   b. gender identity disorder
   c. transvestism
   d. psychosexual dysfunction
7. Efforts to alter gender identity have
   a. been quite successful in most cases through behavioral techniques such as aversive conditioning.
   b. been quite successful in most cases through psychodynamic psychotherapy.
   c. been successful through either behavior therapy or psychodynamic psychotherapy provided the individual is under 13 years of age.
   d. generally not been successful after 18 months of age.
8. The authors suggest that much transvestism can be explained
   a. by the presence of hormonal imbalances.
   b. in terms of conditioning.
   c. as a rebellion against one's own sexual desires.
   d. as part of hallucinations that accompany schizophrenia.
9. Which of the following persons is most likely to engage in voyeurism?
   a. a married woman who is unhappy with her sexual relations
   b. a homosexual man who is "in between" lovers
   c. an adolescent male who is shy and feels dominated by women
   d. an elderly man who lives by himself
10. The most common sexual offense reported to the police is
    a. exhibitionism.
    b. obscene phone calls.
    c. voyeurism.
    d. rape.
11. Most exhibitionists
    a. are adolescents who have never had sexual relations.
    b. are immature married males.
    c. are also aggressive and assaultive.
    d. try to have sexual relations with their victims.
12. Which of the following statements concerning rape is *not* true?
    a. A sizable percentage of rapists' dominant motive is sexual satisfaction.
    b. Most rapists who are arrested are under 25 years of age.
    c. Most rapes are premeditated, planned events.
    d. About half of the arrested rapists are married.
13. In the treatment of variant sexual behavior the authors of the text recommend
    a. assessment of multiple areas of functioning and a broad-based psychological approach.
    b. a symptom-oriented approach with direct modification of specific behavior.
    c. a legal approach, using incarceration as punishment.
    d. a medical approach, using assessment of hormonal balances and chemotherapy.
14. The Kinsey (1948) data on male homosexuality provided evidence for
    a. biological factors in homosexual orientation.
    b. the view that sexual orientation exists on a continuum and not a dichotomy.
    c. a high rate of criminal sexual behavior among homosexuals.
    d. a high rate of personality maladjustment among homosexuals.

15. Money and his associates (1974) have hypothesized that homosexuality in adulthood is related to
    a. genetic factors.
    b. chromosomal aberrations present in utero.
    c. prenatal or early postnatal hormonal influences.
    d. the level of plasma testosterone.

13

Organic mental disorders and mental retardation

OVERVIEW

Most mental disorders do not involve any known brain pathology. Those that do are discussed in this chapter. The chapter is divided into two major divisions: (1) organic mental disorders and (2) mental retardation.

The discussion of organic mental disorders begins with a description of the kinds of symptoms that may be seen as a result of brain pathology. Then, some of the specific causes of brain pathology, such as brain tumors, head injury, old age, etc., are described.

The section on mental retardation discusses the behavior that is characteristic of the different levels or degrees of mental retardation. The various causes of retardation are specified.

Since both mental retardation and organic mental disorders are fairly common, it is important to develop a familiarity with them.

TERMS YOU SHOULD KNOW

organic mental disorders (p. 489)

mental retardation (p. 489)

acute (p. 492)

chronic (p. 492)

acute brain disorder (p. 492)

acute delirium (p. 492)

chronic brain disorder (p. 492)

syndromes (p. 492)

delirium (p. 493)

dementia (p. 494)

amnestic syndrome (p. 494)

confabulation (p. 494)

hallucinosis (p. 494)

organic delusional syndrome (p. 494)

organic affective syndrome (p. 495)

organic personality syndrome (p. 495)

general paresis (p. 496)

chancre (p. 496)

great pox (p. 496)

cluster testing (p. 499)

tumor (p. 500)

malignant (p. 500)

benign (p. 500)

chocked disc (p. 500)

"lilliputian hallucinations" (p. 501)

retrograde amnesia (p. 504)

intracerebral hemorrhage (p. 504)

petechial hemorrhage (p. 504)

senile dementia (p. 505)

presenile dementia (p. 505)

Alzheimer's disease (p. 505)

(Picks' disease) (p. 506)

(Huntington's chorea) (p. 506)

plagues (p. 506)

neurofibrillary tangles (p. 506)

cerebrovascular insufficiency (p. 509)

intracerebral hemorrhage (p. 509)

small stroke (p. 509)

multiple-infarct dementia (p. 509)

cerebrovascular accident (CVA) (p. 509)

aphasic conditions (p. 510)

role obsolescence (p. 514)

expectancies of mutual gratification (p. 515)

mild mental retardation (educable) (p. 518)

moderate mental retardation (trainable) (p. 519)

severe mental retardation (dependent retarded) (p. 519)

profound mental retardation (life support retarded) (p. 519)

anoxia (p. 520)

Down's syndrome (p. 521)

(Tay-Sach's disease) (p. 521)

(Turner's syndrome) (p. 521)

(Klinefelter's syndrome) (p. 521)

(Niemann-Pick's disease) (p. 521)

(bilirubin encephalopathy) (p. 521)

(rubella, congenital) (p. 521)

trisomy (p. 522)

amniocentesis (p. 523)

phenylketonuria (PKU) (p. 523)

cretinism (p. 524)

myxedema (p. 524)

macrocephaly (p. 525)

microcephaly (p. 525)

hydrocephalus (p. 525)

cultural-familial retardation (p. 526)

mainstreaming (p. 531)

CONCEPTS TO MASTER

1. Introduction

   Why does it make a difference whether the brain damage to a patient occurred at birth versus at 16 years of age? (p. 489)

2. Organic mental disorders

   a. What three factors determine the extent of behavioral deficits and psychopathology that will result from brain damage? (p. 490)

      1.

      2.

      3.

   b. On what three grounds would a clinician suspect that a psychosis is caused by underlying organic pathology? (p. 490)

      1.

      2.

      3.

   c. How frequent was organic disease in the survey Hall et al. (1980) conducted among acutely disturbed psychiatric inpatients? How frequent was organic disease among less disturbed patients? (p. 490)

   d. Why can't brain damage just heal as a cut on the hand does? (p. 490)

   e. If certain functions are "knocked out" as a result of brain damage, can they ever be relearned? (p. 490)

   f. Fill in the following chart which summarizes the probable impairment that would result from brain damage in various locations. (pp. 491–492)

Area of the Brain Damaged	Probable Clinical Picture
1. frontal areas	either passivity and apathy or impulsiveness and distractibility
2. right parietal area	
3. left parietal area	
4. temporal area	
5. occipital area	

g. Place the words *acute* and *chronic* where they belong in the blanks in the chart below. (p. 492)

Type of Organic Disorder	Characteristics
A. _____ organic mental disorders	1. Are caused by diffuse impairment of the brain. 2. Causes include high fevers and drug intoxication. 3. Delirium, hallucinations, and stupor predominate clinical picture. 4. Prognosis for recovery is good.
B. _____ organic mental disorders	1. Are caused by permanent destruction of some brain tissue. 2. Impairment of orientation, memory, learning, emotion, and/or ethical controls are predominant symptoms.

e. What three words are used to indicate the severity of a particular case of organic mental disorder? (p. 492)

_____,

_____, and

_____.

183

3. Organic symptom syndromes
   a. The clusters of symptoms based on brain damage listed in the DSM–III are grouped by the authors into four clusters. What are they? (p. 492)
      1.

      2.

      3.

      4.

   b. What processes are most seriously disturbed in dementia? (p. 494)

   c. Match the following:

      1. delirium   a. Caused by repeated strokes, infections, tumors, and injuries.
      2. dementia   b. Caused by head injury, abuse of alcohol or other drugs, and lack of oxygen to the brain.

   d. Which of the following would a person with amnestic syndrome have the most problem remembering? (p. 494)
      1. The name of the doctor who just introduced herself one second before.
      2. What he or she had for breakfast.
      3. Details of his or her childhood from 50 years ago.
   e. Is overall cognitive functioning impaired in the amnestic syndrome as it is in dementia? (p. 494)

   f. Is the most common form of amnestic syndrome, those due to alcohol or barbiturate addiction, considered reversible? (p. 494)

   g. Fill in the following chart which summarizes the most common causes of the following organic syndromes.

184

Organic Syndrome		Common Etiological Factors
1. delirium	(p. 493)	head injury, toxic or metabolic disturbances, oxygen deprivation, insufficient blood to brain, or alcohol and drugs in an addicted person
2. dementia	(p. 494)	
3. amnestic syndrome	(p. 494)	
4. hallucinosis	(p. 494)	
5. affective syndrome	(p. 495)	
6. personality syndrome	(p. 495)	

4. General paresis
   a. The following are the stages in the development of general paresis. Answer the following questions regarding them.
   Stage 1—A chancre appears at the point of contact with the infected person.
   Stage 2—A generalized skin rash appears.
   Stage 3—Spirochetes multiply and are carried in the bloodstream to various parts of the body, but no outward symptoms are observed.
   Stage 4—A wide range of disabilities begin to appear gradually, including mental problems related to brain damage.
   1. How many people who contract syphilis (Stage 1) eventually get general paresis (Stage 4)? (p. 496)

   2. How long does it usually take to progress from Stage 1 to Stage 4? (p. 496)

3. What are the various physical problems that may be seen at stage 4?　　　　　　　(p. 497)

4. What three types of emotional reactions are observed among persons in Stage 4?　　(p. 497)
    1.

    2.

    3.

5. Who is more likely to progress from Stage 1 to general paresis?　　　　　　　　(p. 498)
    1. males or females?

    2. blacks or whites?

6. Are homosexuals and prostitutes a major source of syphilitic infection?　　　　(p. 499)

b. Following are the possible outcomes of treatment for general paresis. Indicate how frequently
    each outcome occurs.　　　　　　　　　　　　　　　　　　　　　　　　　(p. 499)

    _____ percent   1. Death during treatment or within ten years after.
    _____ percent   2. No improvement of the mental and physical impairment.
    _____ percent   3. Some improvement, but individual can no longer handle his or her
                                  previous level of life responsibilities.
    _____ percent   4. Good improvement with resumption of former activities and occu-
                                  pation.

5. Disorder involving brain tumors
    a. The clinical picture seen among individuals with brain tumors is very variable. What two factors
        determine the degree of impairment any given tumor will produce?　　　　　　(p. 500)
        1.

        2.

    b. What is the most frequent early symptom people who were later found to have brain tumors
        experienced?　　　　　　　　　　　　　　　　　　　　　　　　　　　　(p. 500)

c. Describe the usual results of a tumor in the following areas of the brain: (p. 501)
   1. frontal lobe

   2. special sensory areas

   3. temporal lobe.

d. About how many brain tumors are curable? (p. 502)

6. Disorders involving head injury
   a. Why do people with emotional problems often remember a time when they received a blow to the head? (p. 502)

   b. What causes people to experience retrograde amnesia after accidents? (p. 504)

   c. Why is boxing potentially dangerous? (p. 504)

   d. How common is epilepsy after a head injury? (pp. 504–505)

   e. What seven factors in the following short example suggest that the patient has an unfavorable prognosis?
   "An 18-year-old male who had several run-ins with the law during high school received a serious head injury in a motorcycle accident. He was in a coma for almost a month. The patient is currently suffering some paralysis and is very angry and depressed. He refuses to cooperate with his physical therapist. His parents, who live in a remote rural area where no rehabilitation facilities are available, will take him back home but are rather unenthusiastic about the prospect." (p. 505)
   1.

   2.

187

3.

4.

5.

6.

7.

7. Senile and presenile dementias
   a. What are the major differences between senile and presenile dementia?   (p. 505)

   b. Describe the neurological degeneration that occurs in Alzheimer's disease. Why are these findings
       thought to implicate acetylcholine depletion as the most likely cause of the disease?   (p. 506)

   c. How common is Alzheimer's disease   (p. 506)
       1. among persons over 65?

       2. among nursing home residents?

   d. Describe the onset of Alzheimer's disease.   (pp. 506–507)

   e. Alzheimer's disease can take five forms. Label the following graph to indicate the frequency of
       each form.

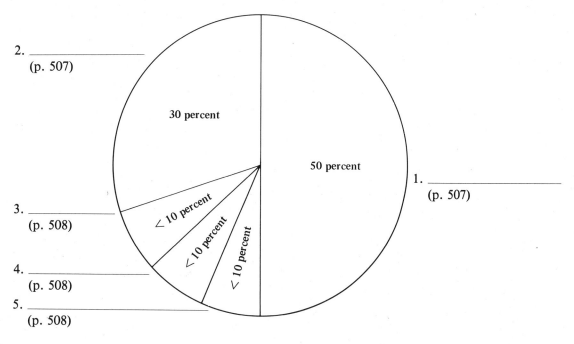

2. _____
   (p. 507)

30 percent

50 percent

< 10 percent

< 10 percent

< 10 percent

1. _____
   (p. 507)

3. _____
   (p. 508)

4. _____
   (p. 508)

5. _____
   (p. 508)

8. Disorders involving cerebral arteriosclerosis
   a. What physical change causes "cerebrovascular insufficiency" and "intracerebral hemorrhage"? (p. 509)

   b. What are the results when a small blood vessel ruptures in the brain? (p. 509)

      What happens when a large blood vessel ruptures?

   c. In about half of the cases, symptoms of cerebral arteriosclerosis appear suddenly. Describe the clinical picture in these cases. (p. 510)

d. Describe the clinical picture in cases where the symptoms of cerebral arteriosclerosis appear gradually. (p. 510)

e. How does the clinical picture in Alzheimer's disease differ from cerebral arteriosclerosis? (pp. 510–511)

9. Causal factors in the psychoses of old age
   a. Is it realistic to consider genetic factors as primary causes of Alzheimer's and arteriosclerotic brain disease? Yes No (p. 512)
   b. Are there reports of Alzheimer's disease showing a familial transmission pattern? Yes No (p. 512)
   c. Gal (1959) did a study in which postmortem examinations were performed on the brains of 104 people who had died naturally of old age. Some of these people had shown signs of seniliform psychoses and some had not. What did Gal find? (p. 512)

   What do these findings suggest about the importance of biological factors in the causal pattern of seniliform psychoses? (p. 512)

   d. The authors of the text discuss several psychosocial factors that play a causal role in seniliform psychoses. The first factor is the patient's prepsychotic personality. Describe the types of personality characteristics that may predispose a person to seniliform psychoses. (p. 512)

   e. It is suggested in the text that negative environmental changes are more harmful to older persons than organic changes. Describe three environmental factors that may prove stressful for older persons. (pp. 512–513)
      1.

      2.

      3.

10. Treatment and outcome for old-age psychoses
    a. Why is hospitalization of the older person showing confusion, depression, etc. considered a last resort? (p. 514)

    b. Many treatments may be helpful for the person with seniliform dementia. List some of these. (p. 514)

    c. Describe what happened on a ward of older men with seniliform psychoses when they were dressed in more formal clothes and given beer every day. (p. 515)

    How did the researchers explain these changes? (p. 515)

    d. List four favorable indications in the following short description that suggest a positive treatment outcome is likely. (p. 516)
    "After his wife's death, a 74-year-old former college professor became increasingly confused and depressed. His children finally had him hospitalized. At the hospital, doctors found minor cerebral arteriosclerosis and no other serious health problems, such as obesity, alcoholism, or hypertension. After his hospitalization, the professor's children planned to send him to an excellent retirement center only blocks from his former university."
       1.

       2.

       3.

       4.

11. Mental retardation
    a. What is the AAMD (American Association on Mental Deficiency) IQ cutoff for mental retardation? (p. 517)

    How many retarded people are there in the United States according to this standard? (p. 517)

    b. Why does the incidence of mental retardation increase markedly at ages five to six? (p. 517)

12. Levels of mental retardation
    a. What is the purpose of IQ tests?   (p. 517)

    b. In addition to an IQ test score lower than 70, what evidence is required to make a diagnosis
       of mental retardation?   (p. 517)

    c. Fill in the missing information in the following chart that summarizes the educational potential,
       level of care required, and the degree of physical deformities characteristic of each level of retardation.

Level of Retardation	Description
Mild (IQ 52–68) (p. 518)	Persons in this group are considered "educatable." They can master simple academic and occupational skills and become self-supporting. Physically, these individuals are normal.
Moderate (IQ 36–51) (p. 519)	Persons in this group are considered _____. They can gain partial independence in self-care, learn acceptable behavior, and work within the family or sheltered workshop. These individuals appear physically ungainly.
Severe (IQ 20–35) (p. 519)	Persons in this group are called "dependent retarded." They can _____ _____ _____. Physical handicaps are common.
Profound (IQ below 20) (p. 519)	Persons in this group are considered _____. They are capable of only the simplest tasks, and speech does not develop. They must remain in custodial care their whole lives. Serious physical deformities are common.

    d. Which levels of retardation can be diagnosed readily in infancy?   (p. 519)

e. The distribution of intelligence should look like a perfect normal curve as shown by Graph A below, but it actually looks like Graph B. Why does this bulge at the lower end of the intelligence distribution, which indicates that there are more mentally retarded people than extremely intelligent people, occur? (p. 519)

A. Theoretical Distribution of Intelligence

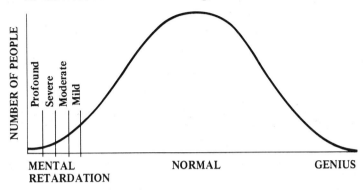

B. Actual Distribution of Intelligence

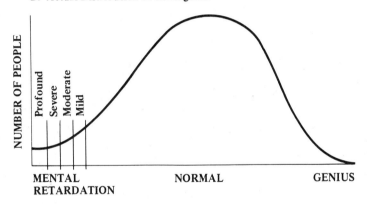

13. Mental retardation and organic brain dysfunction
    a. How frequently is mental retardation associated with known organic pathology? How severe is the retardation in these organic cases? (pp. 519–520)

    b. The authors of the text list five biological conditions that may lead to mental retardation. They are presented below. Briefly describe each one. (pp. 520–521)

1. genetic-chromosomal factors

2. infections and toxic agents

3. prematurity and birth trauma

4. ionizing radiation

5. malnutrition.

c. Describe some of the physical characteristics of children born with Down's syndrome.   (p. 522)

d. Describe the following features of the clinical picture of Down's syndrome:
How common is Down's syndrome?   (p. 521)

How long do these children live?   (p. 521)

What level of mental retardation is usually present in children with Down's syndrome? Is the intellectual defect consistent across abilities? Are these children atypically placid and affectionate?   (p. 522)

e. Down's syndrome is caused by an extra chromosome, number 21. (Normal children have 23 pairs of chromosomes—46 total. Down's syndrome children have 23 pairs also, but "pair" 21 has three chromosomes instead of the normal two—47 total.) Where does the extra chromosome come from?   (pp. 522–523)

The risk of having a child with Down's syndrome is high if the mother is age _____ or older or the father is age _____ or older.   (p. 523)
An obstetrician might order that "amniocentesis" be performed during a pregnancy if parents are older. Why would the physician do this?   (p. 523)

f. Why does a child with phenylketonuria (PKU) appear normal until six to twelve months of age?   (p. 523)

PKU can be identified by a simple test of the infant. Once found, how is PKU treated?   (p. 524)

What level of retardation is likely if PKU goes untreated?   (p. 523)

Cretinism is a form of mental retardation that usually results from malnutrition. What was missing in the diets of cretins?   (p. 524)

How can this form of malnutrition be avoided?   (p. 525)

g. How severely retarded are microcephalic children?   (p. 525)

What are the causes of microcephaly?

h. What is the outcome for hydrocephalic children today?   (p. 526)

14. Mental retardation and sociocultural deprivation
    a. Culturally-familially mentally retarded persons usually fall into the
       _____ level of retardation.   (p. 526)
       The *majority* of all cases of mental retardation are cultural-familial and *not* due to chromosomal
       abnormalities, diseases, radiation, etc.
    b. When is cultural-familial mental retardation usually diagnosed?   (p. 526)

    c. What proportion of mentally retarded children come from socially, economically, and culturally
       deprived homes?   (p. 526)

    d. What three factors usually account for errors in measuring an individual's IQ?   (p. 528)
       1.

       2.

       3.

15. Treatment, outcomes, and prevention
    a. Few retarded children are institutionalized today, but what two types of retarded cihldren are most
       likely to become institutionalized?   (pp. 528–529)
       1.

       2.

    b. Are services for the mentally retarded adequate, and are all affected individuals being reached by
       specialized services?   (p. 529)

    c. List some of the forms of care for the mentally retarded that are alternatives to institutionali-
       zation.   (p. 530)

d. Today, educational training procedures are often based on a behavioral approach. First, an assessment is carried out to determine which areas a person needs to improve. These areas are referred to as target areas. Typical target areas include
_____. (p. 531)
Within each area, the skills the individual needs to learn are broken down to their simplest components, and each component is taught separately.

e. List some of the positive and negative features of the "mainstreaming" approach to the education of retarded children. (p. 531)

f. Prevention of mental retardation is proceeding on two fronts. What are they? (p. 531)
1.

2.

g. List the three areas of emphasis President Kennedy's Committee on Mental Retardation suggested to alleviate sociocultural conditions that deprive children of the stimulation, motivation, and opportunity for normal learning. (p. 531)
1.

2.

3.

h. For what group of youngsters are programs like "Sesame Street" and "The Electric Company" or preschool centers like Head Start designed? What group appears to benefit most? (p. 532)

(16.) Dementia in 417 patients fully evaluated for dementia
In what proportion of cases of dementia is Alzheimer's disease the cause? (p. 495)

(17.) Presenile dementias
What are two presenile dementias other than Alzheimer's disease?   (p. 506)

(18.) Incidence of mental retardation
    a.   Which of the following degrees of retardation is by far the most common?   (p. 517)
        1.   profound
        2.   moderate
        3.   severe
        4.   mild.

(19.) Difficulties of mentally retarded people in learning basic academic skills   (p. 518)
Describe the three major difficulties faced by mentally retarded children in learning basic academic skills.
1.

2.

3.

20.   The wild boy of Aveyron
What was the outcome Pinel achieved after devoting 5½ years to teaching the wild boy?   (p. 527)

21.   Two innovative deinstitutionalization approaches   (p. 530)
Describe how each of the following programs operate.
1.   MORC "Community training homes"

2.   ENCOR houses and apartments.

CHAPTER QUIZ

1. When gross structural defects in the brain occur before birth or at a very early age, the typical result is
   a. mental retardation.
   b. delirium.
   c. dementia.
   d. amnesia.
2. Approximately how many acutely disturbed hospitalized psychiatric parents show the presence of contributory organic disease?
   a. 75 percent
   b. 50 percent
   c. 25 percent
   d. 15 percent.
3. Disturbances in eating, sexuality, and the emotions are associated with damage to the _____ lobe of the brain.
   a. right parietal
   b. frontal
   c. temporal
   d. occipital
4. The inability to remember ongoing events more than a few minutes after they have taken place is called
   a. dementia.
   b. amnestic syndrome.
   c. confabulation.
   d. lilliputian hallucinations.
5. The progressive personality deterioration of general paresis appears during the _____ state of the disease.
   a. first
   b. second
   c. third
   d. fourth
6. The personality deterioration in general paresis takes all the following forms *except*
   a. paranoid.
   b. expansive.
   c. depressed.
   d. demented.
7. The major source of infection in syphillis is
   a. homosexual contact.
   b. heterosexual contact.
   c. prostitutes.
   d. blood transfusions.
8. How many treated paretics can be expected to show a good recovery and resume their former occupation?
   a. 100 percent
   b. 15–25 percent
   c. 20–30 percent
   d. 30–40 percent.

9. The most common symptom in brain tumor cases is
   a. depression.
   b. memory impairment.
   c. restlessness.
   d. headaches.
10. Current theory emphasizes _____ as the most likely cause of Alzheimer's disease.
    a. acetylcholine depletion
    b. dopamine blocking
    c. enkephalin deficit
    d. petechial hemorrhages
11. The most common of the psychotic reactions accompanying Alzheimer's disease takes the form of
    a. simple deterioration.
    b. preshyophrenia.
    c. agitation.
    d. delirium and confusion.
12. Mental retardation is defined as an IQ below 70 and evidence of
    a. brain damage.
    b. birth trauma.
    c. social deprivation.
    d. social incompetence.
13. The most prevalent form of retardation is
    a. mild mental retardation.
    b. moderate mental retardation.
    c. severe mental retardation.
    d. profound mental retardation.
14. A trisomy of chromosome 21 will result in
    a. macrocephalus.
    b. PKU.
    c. Down's syndrome.
    d. hydrocephalus.
15. The most common cause of mental retardation is
    a. genetic factors.
    b. infectious and toxic agents.
    c. prematurity and trauma.
    d. deprivation of normal stimulation.

14

Behavior disorders of childhood and adolescence

OVERVIEW

Many of the mental disorders described in previous chapters do not develop until early or middle adulthood. In dealing with children, the mental health worker is faced with some problems that are unique to childhood, such as hyperactivity, and with others, such as withdrawal, that may be forerunners of serious adult problems with depression or schizoid behavior. The types of problems seen in children are described in this chapter as well as the treatments typically used for each one. In each instance, there is an attempt to indicate what the long-range outcome for the problem usually is. It's important to place emphasis on the treatment of children and adolescent problems, because successful treatment at these stages prevents the occurrence of more serious pathology and spares years of suffering.

TERMS YOU SHOULD KNOW

clinical-nosological strategy (of classification) (p. 537)

multivarite strategy (of classification) (p. 538)

conduct disorder (p. 539)

anxiety-withdrawal (p. 539)

immaturity (p. 539)

socialized aggressive disorder (p. 540)

attention deficit disorder (p. 541)

juvenile delinquency (p. 546)

(minimal brain dysfunction—MBD) (p. 543)

(Ritalin) (p. 545)

(token reinforcement program) (p. 547)

(fading) (p. 547)

social rejects (p. 554)

juvenile status offenders (p. 557)

separation anxiety disorder (p. 558)

avoidant disorder of childhood or adolescence (p. 559)

overanxious disorder (p. 559)

pervasive developmental disorder (p. 562)

infantile autism (p. 562)

echolalia (p. 563)

self-stimulation (p. 563)

structural therapy (p. 565)

eneuresis (p. 567)

encopretic (p. 570)

somnambulism (p. 570)

nail-biting (p. 570)

tics (p. 571)

double deprivation (p. 572)

child advocacy (p. 577)

individual case advocacy (p. 577)

anaclitic depression (p. 559)

(run tos) (p. 551)

(run froms) (p. 551)

(throw aways) (p. 551)

(functional dysphagia) (p. 561)

CONCEPTS TO MASTER

1. Maladaptive behavior in different life periods
    a. Childhood disorders differ from adult disorders on the following three dimensions. Briefly answer the following questions pertaining to these differences.   (p. 536)

Differences between Childhood and Adult Disorders

1. differences in clinical picture (p. 536)	In general, how does the clinical picture in childhood disorders differ from adults?
2. special vulnerability from limited perspective and dependency on adults (p. 536)	What does it mean to say that children have a limited perspective? How is the greater dependency of children on adults an asset? How is it a liability?

2. Classification of childhood and adult disorders
   a. List three problems with early childhood diagnostic systems such as DSM–I and DSM–II.   (p. 537)
      1.

      2.

      3.

   b. See the chart on p. 204. Place a star (*) next to the characteristics that differentiate how these two approaches to classification of childhood disorders operate.

Strategy	Characteristics
clinical-nosological strategy (p. 537)	1. descriptive categories are developed through clinical study 2. based on observation 3. requires presence or absence of symptoms to classify 4. requires few symptoms 5. has many categories
multivariate strategy (p. 538)	1. descriptive categories are developed statistically 2. based on observation 3. requires presence or absence of symptoms to classify 4. requires a number of symptoms 5. has few categories

c. The DSM–III was constructed by the _____ strategy. (p. 538)

d. When diagnosing children, what categories make up Axis I? (p. 538)
   1. mental retardation

   2.

   3.

   4.

   5.

   6.

   7.

What is Axis II used for? What categories make up Axis II? (p. 538)
   1. developmental language disorder

   2.

   3.

   4.

e. Match the following investigators with the diagnostic symptom clusters they created using multivariate strategies.

Investigator		Clusters Identified	
1.	Petersen (1961) (p. 539)	a.	unsocialized aggressive, socialized aggressive, overinhibited
2.	Hewitt and Jenkins (1946) (p. 539)	b.	conduct disorder, anxiety-withdrawal, immaturity, socialized aggressive disorder
3.	Quay (1979) (p. 539)	c.	conduct problems, personality problems

f. Fill in the following two terms in the appropriate blanks to coincide with the proper set of characteristics: clinical-nosological, multivariate.

_____ strategy   _____ strategy   (p. 540)

1. arbitrary classes (Uses presence and absence of symptoms—you're in a diagnostic group or you're not.)	1. classes true to life (Uses numerical scores—everyone falls somewhere on each dimension.
2. focuses on breadth (Some classes are quite rare and may not actually exist.)	2. focuses on depth (Rare symptoms are disregarded; common symptoms are emphasized.)
3. less clarity	3. more clarity

3. Attention deficit disorder
   a. Hyperactivity is the most frequent reason children are referred to mental health facilities. It is estimated that between _____ and _____ percent of elementary school aged children manifest the symptoms of hyperactivity. The disorder occurs with greatest frequency before age _____, although some residual effects may persist until adolescence.   (p. 541)
   b. Describe the clinical picture in hyperactivity in the following areas.
      1. muscular activity   (p. 541)

      2. attention   (p. 541)

      3. impulsive control   (p. 541)

      4. responsibility   (p. 541)

5. intelligence (p. 541)

6. parental relationships (p. 541)

c. Why have researchers concluded that the diagnostic category of hyperactivity has little meaning? (p. 542)

d. Indicate current thinking regarding the following possible causes of hyperactivity:
1. biological basis (p. 542)

2. diet (p. 542)

3. parental personality problems. (p. 542)

e. The authors state that the diagnosis of hyperactivity doesn't really tell you anything much about a child. Why not? (p. 542)

f. Amphetamines, such as Ritalin, have been used to treat hyperactivity. Are they effective? (pp. 543–544)

What possible harmful side effects do they have? (p. 544)

g. What does a behavioral therapy program for hyperactivity involve? (p. 544)

h. Why are cognitive-behavioral techniques used with hyperactive children? What do these techniques accomplish? (p. 544)

i. What treatment approach was identified as most effective by Pelham et al. (1980)? (p. 545)

j. What did Weiss et al. (1979) report regarding the adult adjustment of formerly hyperactive children? (p. 546)

k. Does "attention deficit without hyperactivity" exist? (p. 546)

4. Conduct disorders
    a. The authors conclude that the terms *conduct disorders, early stages of psychopathic personality,* and _____ probably mean the same thing. (p. 547)
    b. The essential symptomatic behavior in conduct disorders is
        _____. (p. 547)
    c. In DSM–III, conduct disorders are subclassified on two dimensions: whether the child had adequate social bonds (socialized versus unsocialized) and whether the child's misbehavior is aggressive or not (_____ versus
        _____). (p. 548)
    d. Describe what is known regarding the following causal factors of conduct disorder: (p. 548)
        1. family setting

        2. institutionalization.

    e. Therapy for conduct disorders is ineffective unless
        _____. (pp. 548–549)
        Fareta (1981) reported that many conduct disordered children grew up to be adults who
        _____. (p. 549)

207

f. How is behavior therapy used to assist the parents of conduct disordered children?   (p. 549)

5. Incidence of delinquency
    a. What happened to the frequency of juvenile crime between 1972 and 1981?   (p. 550)

    b. Does juvenile delinquency occur at a higher rate among males or females?   (p. 550)

        For what crimes are females commonly arrested?   (pp. 550–551)

        For what crimes are males most often arrested?   (p. 551)

    c. Are juveniles frequently violent?   (p. 551)

6. Fill in the missing information on the following chart that summarizes the research on the causal factors of juvenile delinquency.

Causal Factors in Juvenile Delinquency

A. Personal Pathology	
1. genetic determinants (p. 552)	Schulsinger (1972) found adopted psychopathic criminals more often had psychopathic fathers than non-psychopathic criminals.
2. brain damage and mental retardation (p. 552)	Less than _____ percent of delinquents have been found to have brain damage that could lead to lowered inhibitory controls and violent behavior. Some _____ percent of delinquents are found to be mentally retarded and unable to foresee the consequences of their actions or understand the significance of what they are doing.

3. neuroses and psychoses (p. 552)	In a small portion of cases, delinquent acts are performed by a neurotic individual. In this case, the neurotic acts probably represent _____.
4. psychopathic traits (p. 552)	A sizable number of habitual delinquents appear to share traits typical of psychopathic persons, such as _____.
B. Pathogenic Family Patterns	
1. broken homes (p. 553)	Delinquency seems to be more common in homes broken by _____ or _____ than in homes broken by death of a parent.
2. parental rejection (p. 553)	When the father rejects a boy, the following may occur: _____. If the father uses physical punishment, what happens? _____.
3. psychopathic parental models (p. 553)	Psychopathic behaviors found in the fathers of delinquents included: _____. Psychopathic fathers and mothers may contribute to the delinquency of girls by: _____.
4. parental relationships (p. 554)	Children's oppositional behavior (negativism) is greater when parents have few friendly contacts outside the home.
5. undesirable peer relationships (p. 554)	About _____ percent of delinquent acts involved one or two other persons, and most of the remainder involved three or four other persons.
C. General Sociocultural Factors	
1. alienation and rebellion (p. 554)	How may teenagers often view the adult world? _____.

2. social rejects (pp. 554–555)	Institutionalized, teenage, male delinquents have been found to be an average of _____ years retarded in academic progress with a reading level of less than _____ grade.
3. gang cultures (p. 556)	What type of feelings does belonging to a gang give a delinquent? _____ _____.
4. unusual stress (p. 556)	How often did unusually stressful events occur shortly before a delinquent act was committed? _____ _____.

7. Dealing with delinquency
   a. Describe what was done by the California Youth Authority in their five-year experiment called "The Community Treatment Project." (pp. 556–557)

   What results were obtained at the 15-month follow-up?

   How did these results compare to data from the control group?

   b. What is the overall recidivism rate for juvenile offenders as estimated by *Time* magazine? (p. 557)

8. Anxiety disorders of childhood and adolescence
   a. Jenkins (1968) reported that about 20 percent of disturbed children were suffering problems of anxiety and withdrawal. _____ were most commonly affected. (p. 558)
   b. Children with anxiety disorders share seven general characteristics. List them. (p. 558)
      1.

      2.

      3.

      4.

5.

6.

7.

c. Separation anxiety disorder
In most cases of separation anxiety a clear psychological stress triggered the symptoms.
True or False   (p. 558)
d. Avoidant disorder of childhood or adolescence
Because these children withdraw from the real world their capacity to
_____ deteriorates. Avoidant children are charac-
terized by _____
_____. (p. 559)

e. Overanxious disorder
Here the anxiety may be in the form of fears, _____ problems, or
sleeping problems. (p. 559)
f. Causal factors of anxiety and avoidant disorders include:
1. easy conditionability and a build-up of _____
2. undermining of self-adequacy by _____
3. the modeling by an overanxious parent who sensitizes the child to
   _____
4. detached parents who fail to _____
5. inadequate relationships.
g. As growth into adolescence and adulthood occurs, what happens to anxious and avoidant problems? (p. 560)

h. Desensitization using imagination is limited in application to children because _____
_____. (pp. 561–562)
However, _____ methods using graded real life situations can
be effective. (p. 562)

9. Pervasive developmental disorders (infantile autism)
a. Autism may be diagnosed in a child as young as a few _____ old but is almost always diagnosed before _____ years of age. (p. 562)
b. Complete the following chart by writing a brief description of autistic children's behavior in each area.

Area of Behavior	Characteristics of Autistic Children
1. interactions with parents (p. 563)	
2. use of speech (p. 563)	
3. self-stimulation (p. 563)	
4. interactions with objects (p. 563)	
5. concept of self (p. 564)	

c. Circle yes, no, or maybe as appropriate to indicate whether each of the following factors is currently thought to be an important cause of autism:
1. brain pathology   Yes   No   Maybe   (p. 564)
2. chromosome abnormalities   Yes   No   Maybe   (p. 564)
3. subtle constitutional defects   Yes   No   Maybe   (p. 564)
4. personality characteristics of parents.   Yes   No   Maybe   (pp. 564–565)

d. Bartak et al. (1973), at the Maudsley Hospital, compared three different approaches to treating autism: an approach emphasizing formal schooling, a structured form of play therapy, and free play therapy. Which approach was found to be most successful?   (p. 565)

e. How have parents been used as therapists to treat their own autistic children?   (pp. 566–567)

f. What is the prognosis for autism in children who show symptoms before age 2?   (p. 567)

How many children who receive treatment attain a marginal adjustment in adulthood?   (p. 567)

10. Other symptom disorders
    a. Eneuresis
       Surveys of children in medical centers have found _____ percent were
       eneuretic.   (p. 567)
       What are the three major causes of eneuresis?   (p. 567)
       1.

       2.

       3.

       What procedures have proven successful in the treatment of eneuresis? Describe how this treatment
       is conducted.   (p. 567)

       What happens to the incidence of eneuresis as the child gets older if untreated?   (p. 567)

    b. Encopresis
       Respond true or false to the following.
       Regular soiling after age 3 is encopresis.   True   False   (p. 570)
       One third of encopretic children are eneuretic.   True   False   (p. 570)
       Six times more boys than girls are encopretic.   True   False   (p. 570)
       A common time for encopresis is after school.   True   False   (p. 570)
       Most children know they need to have a bowel movement.   True   False   (p. 570)
       What physical problem is often present in encopretic children?   (p. 570)

    c. Sleepwalking (somnambulism)
       How have researchers determined that sleepwalking is related to an anxiety-arousing situation
       and not to acting out of a dream?   (p. 570)

    d. Nail-biting
       How does nail-biting operate as a tension reducer in anxiety-arousing situations?   (pp. 570–571)
       Which of the following methods are successful in treating nail-biting?   (p. 571)
       1. restraint   Yes   No
       2. bitter chemicals painted on fingers   Yes   No
       3. helping child to feel more adequate and secure   Yes   No
       4. behavior therapy   Yes   No

213

e. Tics
Tics usually stem from _____ or _____
in social situations. (p. 572)

11. Special factors associated with treatment for children
    a. In what ways do children have difficulty seeking assistance for emotional problems? (p. 572)

    b. What does it mean to say a child from a pathogenic home is "double deprived"? (p. 572)

    c. What is meant by the expression, "using parents as 'change agents' "? (p. 573)

    d. Give some reasons that placement of a child in a foster home often works out less than ideally
       for the child. (p. 573)

12. Child-advocacy programs
    a. In 1970 the National Institute of Mental Health estimated that fewer than _____ percent
       of disburbed children in the United States were receiving any kind of help, and only half of those
       receiving help were receiving adequate treatment. (p. 576)

13. How prevalent are psychological disorders among children?
    The most realistic estimates suggest that _____ percent of the children in the United
    States are maladjusted. The rate in Great Britain is approximately the same. Maladjustment is
    significantly more common among boys. (p. 536)

14. Minimal brain dysfunction (MBD)
    a. Describe the characteristics of children with MBD. (p. 543)

    b. What is the major criticism of the diagnosis of MBD? (p. 543)

c. What did Edwards et al. (1971) find about the relationship of MBD to school performance? (p. 543)

d. What is accomplished by labeling a child as suffering from "minimal brain dysfunction"? (p. 543)

15. Drug therapy with children
a. What criticism has been made about the way children are selected to receive drugs? (p. 545)

b. What criticism has been made about the purposes for which drugs are used in children? (p. 545)

c. What do we know about the long-range side effects of drug therapy on children? (p. 545)

(16.) Token reinforcement programs in the classroom
a. How do these programs work? (p. 547)

b. How is "fading" accomplished? (p. 547)

c. What behavioral problems are positively affected by token reinforcement? (p. 547)

(17.) Problems that lead children to run away
a. What is the average age of a runaway child? (p. 550)

b. Of runaways reported to the police, _____ percent are eventually located. (p. 551)
c. Is it common for parents of a runaway child to fail to call the police? (p. 551)

18. Television and violence
   a. Describe the findings of Lefkowitz et al. (1977).   (p. 555)

   b. Does this study prove a direct causal link between violence and TV?   (p. 555)

   c. How can TV be viewed as a "precipitating cause of aggressive behavior"?   (p. 555)

(19.) Does childhood depression exist as a clinical syndrome?
   a. List the points made by each side of the controversy over childhood depression. (p. 559)

Evidence Childhood Depression Exists	Evidence Against the Existence of Childhood Depression

(20.) Childhood schizophrenia
   a. How does childhood depression differ from autism?   (p. 564)

   b. What is the prognosis for a child with schizophrenia compared to autism?   (p. 564)

(21.) The problem of child abuse in contemporary society
   a. How often does child abuse result in serious injury?   (p. 574)

b. The most frequent cases of child abuse involve children under _____ years of age. (p. 574)

c. What proportion of children have suffered serious abuse according to Gelles (1978)? (p. 574)

d. What differences emerge when abused children are compared to nonabused children? (p. 574)

e. What common factors have been found among families with abusing parents? (p. 575)

f. Describe the study of high risk families for child abuse. What has been learned so far? (p. 575)

g. Describe the various approaches to prevention of child abuse that are available. (p. 575)

    1.

    2.

    3.

    4.

    5.

(22.) Freeing children for permanent placement
    a.   Describe the project undertaken in Oregon at the Regional Research Unit.   (p. 576)

    b.   What changes in usual procedure were made for purposes of the study?   (p. 576)

CHAPTER QUIZ

1. Early diagnostic systems for childhood disorders have been criticized as inadequate for all the following *except*
   a. too little emphasis on the differences in the clinical picture between child disorders and adult disorders.
   b. lack of continuity between child diagnostic categories and adult categories.
   c. failure to recognize the importance of environmental factors.
   d. lack of attention to normal developmental changes.
2. DSM-III classification of children's disorders was developed by the _____ approach.
   a. epidemiological
   b. empirical
   c. multivariate
   d. clinical nosological
3. Immaturity as a cluster of childhood symptomatology is reflected in such behavior as
   a. fighting, temper tantrums.
   b. anxiety, withdrawal.
   c. daydreaming, clumsy behavior, passivity.
   d. stealing, keeping late hours.
4. The multivariate strategy of diagnostic classification results in
   a. narrow categories.
   b. disorders classified by few symptoms.
   c. attention to rare disorders.
   d. a few clear categories.
5. The most effective treatment for hyperactivity is
   a. behavioral treatment.
   b. tranquilizers.
   c. behavioral intervention and psychostimulants.
   d. no treatment is effective.
6. Youth under 18 account for _____ percent of arrests for robbery.
   a. 5
   b. 10
   c. 33
   d. 50

7. Which of the following causal factors of juvenile delinquency appears to account for a sizable number of cases?
   a. genetic determinants
   b. mental retardation
   c. neuroses and psychoses
   d. psychopathic traits
8. Anxiety disorders appear to represent about _____ percent of childhood disorders.
   a. 10
   b. 20
   c. 30
   d. 40
9. Most cases of separation disorder are related to
   a. undesirable peer pressure.
   b. parental rejection.
   c. psychosocial stressors such as death of a pet.
   d. pathogenic family patterns.
10. What biological cause is thought to be related to anxiety and avoidant disorders?
    a. unusual constitutional sensitivity
    b. exposure to ionizing radiation
    c. low intelligence
    d. high need for stimulation
11. A five-year-old boy, when spoken to, turns his head away, mumbles unintelligibly, and is neither toilet trained nor able to feed himself. Most likely, he would be diagnosed as having
    a. anxiety disorder.
    b. withdrawal disorder.
    c. echolalia
    d. autism
12. Habitual involuntary discharge of urine after age 3 is referred to as
    a. encopresis.
    b. eneuresis.
    c. echolalia.
    d. echopraxia.
13. Treatment without parental consent can occur in all the following cases except
    a. mature minors.
    b. emancipated minors.
    c. emergency situations.
    d. life-threatening illnesses.
14. The trend in the placement of children displaying psychological needs is toward
    a. immediate permanent resolution of home placement.
    b. temporary placement in foster homes.
    c. the use of halfway houses and small group homes.
    d. incorporation of these children into training schools with delinquents.
15. A relatively new approach to child mental health, in which adults work on behalf of children to obtain needed services, is called
    a. primary prevention.
    b. the child guidance movement.
    c. child advocacy.
    d. placement by proxy.

15
Clinical assessment

OVERVIEW

The clinical assessment process is described in this chapter. Clinical assessment includes the use of psychological tests but also depends on data from other sources, such as observation and interview. Psychological tests have a mystique in our society and have recently come under serious public scrutiny. Questions regarding the validity of tests as predictors of academic performance have been raised. Also, concerns have been voiced publicly that tests may invade privacy and reveal things about an individual that he or she did not realize were being revealed. Chapter 15 describes what the different types of tests are, how they are constructed, and what types of information can be obtained from them. The chapter concludes with a discussion of how assessment information is put together with data obtained by other members of the clinical team.

TERMS YOU SHOULD KNOW

clinical assessment (p. 583)

dynamic formulation (p. 585)

electroencephalogram (EEG) (p. 586)

dysrhythmias (p. 586)

computerized axial tomography (CAT scan) (p. 586)

positron emission tomography (PET scan) (p. 586)

neurophychological test battery (p. 587)

Halsted-Reitan battery (p. 587)

(halo effect) (p. 587)

(performance test) (p. 587)

(personality profile) (p. 587)

(test reliability) (p. 587)

(test validity) (p. 587)

(verbal test) (p. 587)

structured interview (p. 590)

observational rating scales (p. 591)

Brief Psychiatric Rating Scale (BPRS)

self-report (p. 591)

role playing (p. 591)

self-monitoring (p. 591)

psychological tests (p. 592)

WISC-R (p. 592)

Stanford-Binet (p. 592)

WAIS-R (p. 592)

personality tests (pp. 592 & 593)

projective tests (p. 593)

Rorschach Test (p. 593)

Thematic Apperception Test (TAT) (p. 594)

sentence completion tests (p. 594)

objective tests (p. 595)

Minnesota Multiphasic Personality Inventory (MMPI) (p. 595)

validity scales (p. 596)

clinical scales (p. 596)

special scales (p. 596)

content interpretation (p. 596)

factor analysis (p. 596)

Sixteen Personality Factor Questionnaire (16PF) (p. 597)

actuarial procedures (p. 606)

automated clinician program (p. 606)

CONCEPTS TO MASTER

1. Introduction
   a. The goal of clinical assessment is to identify and understand an individual's
      _____ within the context of his or her overall
      level of _____ and
      _____.
      (p. 583)
   b. Data from clinical assessment is used for two purposes. First, it serves as a basis for treatment
      decisions. Later, after treatment has begun, it can serve as a _____
      against which to evaluate progress.
      (p. 584)

2. The information sought in assessment
   a. The first step in assessment is for the clinician to determine the
      _____.
      (p. 584)
   b. Why is a formal diagnosis often required on a patient?
      (p. 584)

      For clinical purposes, however, knowledge about an individual's _____,
      _____, personality characteristics, and environmental pressures and re-
      sources is more important.
      (p. 584)
   c. The material gained through assessment is integrated into a consistent and meaningful picture
      that should lead to an explanation of why the person is engaging in maladaptive behavior;
      it should lead to hypotheses about the person's _____
      behavior as well.
      (p. 584)
3. Interdisciplinary sources of assessment data
   What assessment techniques would be favored by a
   (pp. 585–586)
   1. biologically oriented clinician?

   2. psychoanalytically oriented clinician?

   3. behaviorally oriented clinician?

   4. humanistically oriented clinician?

4. Physical evaluation
    a. Medical examinations are necessary in some situations to rule out physical abnormalities or to determine the extent to which physical problems are involved. The two types of medical examinations that may be performed include the _____ examination and the _____ examination.   (p. 586)
    b. List several diagnostic procedures that might be obtained as part of a specialized neurological exam.   (pp. 586–587)

    c. Sometimes psychological tests will be used to detect the presence of organic damage or disease. These tests are referred to as a _____ test battery.   (p. 587)
    d. The Halstead-Reitan is a highly regarded neurophychological test. However, if time is at a premium, the _____ could be used.   (p. 587)

5. Assessment interview
    a. Describe how a clinical interview is usually conducted.   (pp. 588–589)

    b. Why has the clinical interview been criticized as a source of information on which to base clinical decisions?   (p. 589)

    c. How do judgments based on the use of structured interviews and rating scales compare to the accuracy of judgments based on a clinical interview?   (p. 590)

6. Clinical observation
    a. List some different situations in which an individual patient's behavior may be observed directly to obtain information relevant to the assessment process.   (p. 590)

    b. How can rating scales improve clinical observation?   (p. 590)

c. How did Paul and his colleagues (1977, 1978, 1979, 1982) use observational rating
   scales? (pp. 590–591)
d. Jones, Reid, and Patterson (1975) have developed a method of coding and quantifying observa-
   tions of _____ at _____.
   This provides the clinician with information about the _____ that
   are controlling the child's _____. (p. 591)
e. Describe how the following techniques are used to obtain observational data:
   1. role playing (p. 591)

   2. self-monitoring. (p. 591)

7. Psychological tests
   a. Psychological tests are standardized sets of procedures to obtain samples of a subject's behavior
      that can be compared to the behavior of other individuals usually through the use of
      test _____. (p. 592)
   b. Among the characteristics about which the clinician can draw inferences from psychological tests
      are intellectual capacity, _____. (p. 592)
   c. Match the following psychological tests with the appropriate description of each test's purpose.

1. Rorschach Test	(p. 593)	a. rating scale based on standardized inter-
2. Thematic Apperception	(p. 593)	view
Test (TAT)	(p. 594)	b. intelligence scale for children
3. Minnesota Multiphasic Personality Inven-		c. intelligence scale for adults
tory (MMPI)	(p. 595)	d. projective test using inkblots
4. WAIS-R	(p. 592)	e. projective test using pictures
5. WISC-R	(p. 592)	f. structured personality test
6. Brief Psychiatric Rating Scale (BPRS)		g. personality test for normal subjects
	(p. 590)	h. test that pinpoints topics that should be
7. 16PF	(p. 597)	explored
8. Sentence Completion Test (SCT)	(p. 594)	

   d. Individual intelligence tests
      In what type of cases would an individual intelligence test be indicated? In which cases would an
      individual intelligence test be unnecessary? (p. 592)

e. There are basically two kinds of personality tests. What are they?   (p. 593)
    1.

    2.

f. Explain how projective personality tests are assumed to work.   (p. 593)

g. The Rorschach Test
    Which of the following are among the reasons that the use of the Rorschach Test has declined
    over the last 20 years? Circle the correct response.

    1. The Rorschach takes too long to administer.   Yes No   (p. 593)
    2. The Rorschach is often of low or negligible validity except in
        the hands of a skilled interpreter.   Yes No   (p. 594)
    3. The results of the Rorschach are unreliable.   Yes No   (p. 593)
    4. The Rorschach results in behavioral description rather
        than in a formulation of personality dynamics.   Yes No   (p. 593)

h. The Thematic Apperception Test
    The TAT has been criticized for its dated pictures, lengthy administration, and
    _____.   (p. 594)

i. The Minnesota Multiphasic Personality Inventory
    Place a 1, 2, or 3 in front of the following steps to indicate the sequence in which the step
    appeared during the construction of the MMPI.   (p. 596)

    _____ Scales are constructed.
    _____ Item analyses are performed.
    _____ Items are administered to large groups of normal subjects and psychiatric
                  patients.

    What is a validity scale for?   (p. 596)

    How is the MMPI used as a diagnostic standard?   (p. 596)

What criticisms have been made of the MMPI? (p. 596)

j. The Sixteen Personality Factor Questionnaire
    The 16PF was constructed by factor analysis. What does this mean? (pp. 596–597)

k. Complete the chart below that compares the overall strengths and weaknesses of projective and objective tests.

	Strengths	Weaknesses
projective (p. 595)		Interpretations are subjective, unreliable, and difficult to validate, require trained staff to administer and score.
objective (p. 598)	cost effective, reliable, objective, administered and scored by computer	

8. Integration of assessment data
    a. In a clinic or hospital setting, assessment data is usually evaluated in a
        _____ attended by members of the interdisciplinary
        team, including _____ who are concerned with the decision to be
        made regarding treatment. (p. 604)
    b. Fill in the missing data in the following diagram that summarizes the information that is
        utilized in formulating a diagnostic assessment. (pp. 586–592)

    _____physical evaluation_____   +   ____assessment interviews____
    (general physical exam, neurological exam)

                                               +   _____
                                                    (utilizing rating scales in
                                                    environment or hospital)

    and/or _____   =   diagnostic formulation and
            (utilizing structured or unstructured approaches)   treatment plan

226

(9.) The use of computers in assessment
  a. In what respect is a computer "superior to the individual clinician"? (p. 606)

  b. Why might a computer report describe an individual as "responsible" in one paragraph and "irresponsible and impulsive" in another paragraph? (p. 606)

  c. So far, actuarial systems have been developed for only 20 personality types out of the approximately 60 different types seen in a clinical setting. What does the computer do when it is given scores for one of these unstudied types? (p. 606)

  d. In what types of clinical settings is computerized assessment particularly valuable? (p. 606)

(10.) Neuropsychological examination: determining brain-behavior relationships
  a. Match the following subtests of the Halstead-Reitan neuropsychology battery with the correct description of its purpose.

  1. Halstead category test
  2. tactual performance test
  3. rhythm test
  4. speech sounds perception test
  5. finger oscillation test

  a. Determines if an individual can identify spoken words.
  b. Measures a patient's ability to learn and remember.
  c. Gives clues to the extent and location of brain damage.
  d. Measures attention and sustained concentration.
  e. Measures motor speed, response to the unfamiliar, and the learning of tactile and kinesthetic cues.

(11.) Limitations of psychological assessment
  a. Describe *how* each of the following factors *may* limit the accuracy of psychosocial assessment.
    1. cultural bias

    2. overemphasis on internal traits

    3. theoretical orientation of the clinician

227

CHAPTER QUIZ

1. The first step in clinical assessment is
   a. planning a treatment program.
   b. identifying sources of psychopathology.
   c. identifying a problem area.
   d. labeling the disorder according to DSM criteria.

2. A psychologist, in assessing a client, puts together a description of the general behavior and situation of the client and integrates it into a picture that meaningfully explains why the pattern of behavior exists. This description and integration is often referred to as a
   a. dynamic formulation.
   b. Rorschach analysis.
   c. psychoanalysis.
   d. comprehensive diagnosis.

3. A neurological diagnostic aid that reveals how an organ is functioning by measuring metabolic processes is the
   a. PET scan.
   b. CAT scan.
   c. EEG.
   d. angiogram.

4. An abnormal brain wave pattern revealed by an EEG is called a(n)
   a. alpha wave.
   b. brain tumor.
   c. dysrhythmia.
   d. isotope.

5. If a clinical researcher wanted to group patients into treatment groups on the basis of similarity of clinical symptoms, he or she could easily use the
   a. Thematic Apperception Test (TAT).
   b. Brief Psychiatric Rating Scale (BPRS)
   c. Record of Clinical Behavior (RCB).
   d. Rorschach test.

6. The following is an example of such a _____; the observer would check the most appropriate alternative.
   Sexual behavior:

   _____ 1. sexually assaultive: aggressively approaches males or females with sexual intent.

   _____ 2. sexually soliciting: exposes genitals with sexual intent, makes overt sexual advances to other patients or staff, masturbates openly.

   a. structured interview
   b. rating scale
   c. projective test
   d. objective test

7. An instrument used to measure the present level of intellectual functioning in adults is the
   a. WICS-R.
   b. WAIS-R.
   c. TAT.
   d. MMPI.

8. Personality tests are often grouped into two categories,
   a. projective and structured.
   b. behavioral and psychodynamic.
   c. conscious and unconscious.
   d. verbal and performance.
9. The aim of a projective test is to
   a. predict a patient's future behavior.
   b. compare a patient's responses to those of persons who are known to have mental disorders.
   c. assess the role of organic factors in a patient's thinking.
   d. assess how a patient perceives ambiguous stimuli.
10. The use of the Rorschach has decreased recently for all the following reasons *except*
    a. it takes several hours to administer.
    b. the results are often unreliable because of the subjective nature of the interpretations.
    c. more specific behavior descriptions than the Rorschach offers are needed for the types of clinical treatments used in mental health facilities.
    d. there is a dated quality to the test stimuli.
11. All of the following are structured personality tests *except* the
    a. MMPI.
    b. Q Sort.
    c. Sixteen Personality Factor Questionnaire.
    d. TAT.
12. A clinical researcher devises a new psychological test that assesses neuroticism. She is concerned with the possibility that some individuals might not answer the questions in a straightforward, accurate way. To determine whether an individual is honest, she should
    a. factor analyze the responses.
    b. make use of actuarial interpretation.
    c. construct a validity scale.
    d. test the instrument on a group of college students.
13. Advantages of the MMPI and other self-report inventories include all the following except
    a. they are cost effective.
    b. they are highly reliable and objective.
    c. in the hands of a skilled interpreter they can be quite useful in uncovering psychodynamic problems.
    d. they can be administered, scored, and interpreted by computers.
14. Actuarial interpretation is most often used with the
    a. Rorschach test.
    b. TAT.
    c. Q Sort.
    d. MMPI.
15. The most dramatic innovation in clinical assessment during the last decade has been the
    a. development of factor analysis.
    b. use of computers.
    c. introduction of the MMPI.
    d. introduction of the interdisciplinary approach.

16

Biologically based therapies

OVERVIEW

Many states have passed laws during the past few years allowing or requiring pharmacies to post prices for the most frequently used prescription drugs in order to help consumers comparison shop. When such signs were posted, it surprised quite a few people to learn that several of the most frequently used drugs are chemicals that alter the emotional state and not drugs for "physical disease." Because of this widespread use of psychoactive drugs, an informed person should have some understanding of what such drugs can really accomplish and the trade-offs involved in using them.

Chapter 16 presents details about the major types of drugs used for mental disorders: antianxiety, antipsychotic, antidepressant, and antimania, discussing their major effects, side effects, modes of action, and effectiveness. Other biological treatments, such as electric shock and psychosurgery, are also described briefly.

TERMS YOU SHOULD KNOW

insulin shock therapy (p. 610)

electroconvulsive therapy (ECT) (p. 611)

unilateral ECT (p. 613)

prefrontal lobotomy (p. 613)

pharmacology (p. 614)

psychotropic drugs (p. 615)

antipsychotic compounds (major tranquilizers) (p. 615)

chlorpromazine (Thorazine) (p. 615)

tardive dyskinesia (p. 616)

antidepressant compounds (p. 618)

tricyclics (p. 618)

tetracyclics (p. 620)

antianxiety compounds (minor tranquilizers) (p. 620)

benzodiazepines (p. 620)

lithium (p. 621)

megavitamin therapy (p. 625)

orthomolecular approach (p. 626)

hemodialysis (p. 626)

CONCEPTS TO MASTER

1. Early attempts at biological intervention
    a. List several treatments in medicine that involve substantial disruption of biological processes (and suffering to the patient). (p. 610)

2. Coma and convulsive therapies
    a. Insulin coma therapy is no longer practiced. Why was it abandoned? (p. 610)

    b. Describe what happens during ECT. (p. 611)

    c. What are some of the side effects of ECT? (pp. 611–612)

    d. Why did the citizens of Berkeley, California try to ban ECT? (p. 612)

    e. In what kinds of cases might ECT be beneficial? (p. 612)

231

f. What is the latest theory of how ECT works?   (p. 612)

g. What is unilateral ECT? Is it widely employed?   (p. 613)

h. Why is ECT used less frequently today than in the past?   (p. 613)

3. Psychosurgery
    a. After initial enthusiasm, doctors began to recognize that the results of psychosurgery could be very undesirable. What are some of the undesirable results that were found?   (p. 613)

    b. The discovery of _____ caused an almost immediate stop to psychosurgical procedures.   (p. 613)
    c. Today, psychosurgery is used only as a last resort and only in certain specific types of cases. Describe an instance where psychosurgery might be considered as a last resort.   (pp. 613–614)

    d. In the mid 1970s the United States Congress conducted a special investigation into the effects of psychosurgery. What did it conclude?   (p. 614)

4. Emergence of pharmacological methods
    a. During what time period did real progress in the development of chemical compounds for the management of behavioral problems begin?   (p. 614)

5. Types of drugs used
    a. Fill in the missing information in the following chart that summarizes the four types of drugs commonly used for mental disorders.

Class of Drugs	Biological Effect	Behavioral Effect	Example
1. antipsychotics (p. 615)		reduce the intensity of schizophrenic symptoms (including delusions and hallucinations) and have a calming effect	Thorazine
2. antidepressant-tricyclics (p. 618)	Increase concentration of biogenic amines at synapses.		
3. antianxiety-benzodiazepines (p. 620)	Selectively diminish generalized fear.		
4. lithium (pp. 621–622)		resolve 70 percent of manic episodes and may also be useful in depression of bipolar type	

b. Antipsychotic compounds
Below is a schematic diagram of the antipsychotic class of drugs that illustrates the two general types of antipsychotics, official clinical names for these drugs, and the trade names under which they are sold in the drugstore (by prescription only). Fill in the missing trade names.

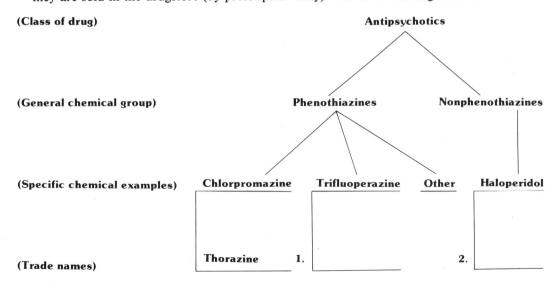

233

In what ways are the behavioral results of treatment with antipsychotic drugs "less than impressive"?

(pp. 616–617)

c. Antidepressant compounds

Below is a schematic diagram of the antidepressant class of drugs that illustrates the three general types of antidepressants, the official chemical names for these drugs, and the trade names under which they are sold in the drugstore (by prescription only). Fill in the missing trade names.

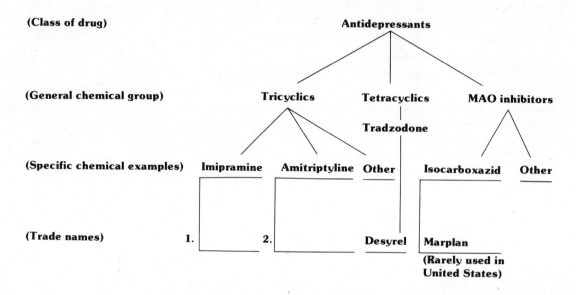

What would probably be done with the patient who fails to respond to either type of antidepressant?

(p. 618)

Antidepressant drugs often produce dramatic improvements in the treated groups. However, what is often observed in untreated depressed people that requires claims for antidepressant drugs to be modest?

(p. 620)

d. Antianxiety compounds

A schematic diagram follows of the antianxiety class of drugs that illustrates the three general types of antianxiety drugs, the official chemical names for the drugs, and the trade names under which they are sold in the drugstore (by prescription only). Fill in the missing information next to numbers 1, 2, 3, and 4.

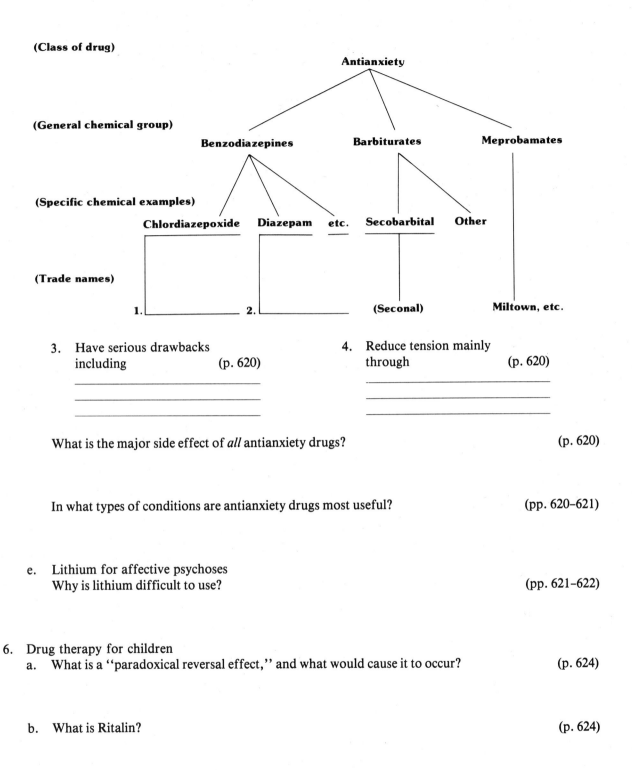

(Class of drug)   **Antianxiety**

(General chemical group)   **Benzodiazepines**   **Barbiturates**   **Meprobamates**

(Specific chemical examples)

           Chlordiazepoxide   **Diazepam**   **etc.**   **Secobarbital**   **Other**

(Trade names)

           1.   2.   **(Seconal)**   **Miltown, etc.**

3. Have serious drawbacks
   including   (p. 620)

   _____
   _____
   _____

4. Reduce tension mainly
   through   (p. 620)

   _____
   _____
   _____

What is the major side effect of *all* antianxiety drugs?   (p. 620)

In what types of conditions are antianxiety drugs most useful?   (pp. 620–621)

e. Lithium for affective psychoses
   Why is lithium difficult to use?   (pp. 621–622)

6. Drug therapy for children
   a. What is a "paradoxical reversal effect," and what would cause it to occur?   (p. 624)

   b. What is Ritalin?   (p. 624)

235

    c.   Why is drug treatment for hyperactivity often stopped during adolescence?   (pp. 624–625)

7.   A perspective on pharmacological therapy
    Does drug therapy cure mental disorders?   (p. 625)

8.   Other biological therapies
    a.   What conclusion did the American Psychiatric Association reach regarding the effectiveness of megavitamin therapy for schizophrenia?   (p. 626)

    b.   What is the latest information available on the effectiveness of hemodialysis as a treatment for schizophrenia?   (p. 626)

9.   Will Alzheimer's disease yield to drug treatment?
    a.   Why is it difficult to treat chemical imbalances in the brain?   (p. 616)

    b.   What is the result of administration of physostigmine?   (p. 616)

    c.   What is the result of administration of naloxone?   (p. 616)

10. Chemically induced sleep: is it worth the risks?
    a.   How did the Institute of Medicine evaluate the safety of the benzodiazepines (e.g. Valium, Librium, Dalmane) as sleeping medication?   (p. 621)

    b.   Should older people who complain of insomnia be given sleeping pills?   (p. 621)

CHAPTER QUIZ

1. Passing a 160-volt electric current through an individual's head will cause all of the following *except*
   a. prolonged coma.
   b. immediate loss of consciousness.
   c. tonic and clonic seizures.
   d. memory impairment and disorientation.
2. Criticisms of the use of ECT for depression include all the following *except*
   a. it is ineffective.
   b. benefits may be short-lived.
   c. it causes demonstrable brain damage.
   d. it is undertaken too routinely.
3. The great majority of psychiatrists employ an unnecessarily damaging, inefficient form of ECT. Which of the following treatments is still effective, but without as many distressing side effects as the damaging, outdated method?
   a. ECT accompanied by muscle stimulants
   b. bilateral ECT
   c. unilateral ECT
   d. cerebellar ECT
4. The widespread use of prefrontal lobotomies declined with the advent of
   a. ECT.
   b. antipsychotic drugs.
   c. behavior therapy.
   d. the community mental health system.
5. Contemporary uses of psychosurgery include
   a. treatment of "psychic pain."
   b. reduction of depression.
   c. modification of schizophrenia.
   d. treatment of some forms of retardation.
6. Roger is a 24-year-old hospitalized male who has recently developed recurring hallucinations and delusions. He would be most likely to benefit from
   a. ECT.
   b. imipramine.
   c. chlorpromazine.
   d. lithium.
7. Which of the following is a trade name for a major antipsychotic drug?
   a. Haldol
   b. Valium
   c. Dyserl
   d. Synaquon
8. The depletion of brain acetylcholine, which sometimes follows the ingestion of antipsychotic drugs, causes a disturbance of motor control called
   a. Korsakoff's psychosis.
   b. MAO inhibition.
   c. tardive dyskinesia.
   d. fluphenazine.

9. Pharmacological treatment of depression with tricyclics is believed to
   a. reduce central nervous system arousal.
   b. reduce intracranial pressure by absorbing cerebral spinal fluid.
   c. increase the availability of lithium in the central nervous system for absorption.
   d. increase the concentration of seritonin and norephinephrine at synaptic sites.

10. One of the most commonly used tricyclic drugs in the treatment of depression is
    a. methylpenidate (Ritalin).
    b. imipramine (Tofranil).
    c. chlordiazepoxide (Librium).
    d. haloperidol (Haldol).

11. A drug that selectively diminishes conditioned fears is
    a. Librium.
    b. Miltown.
    c. Equanil.
    d. Thorazine.

12. Lithium compounds are used in the treatment of
    a. anxiety.
    b. hyperactivity and specific learning disabilities.
    c. bipolar affective psychosis.
    d. hallucinations and delusions.

13. Barry is a six-year-old boy who is causing many problems for his first-grade teacher. He refuses to sit in his seat, he is easily distracted by events outside the window, and he is not learning to read as quickly as the other children. The teacher complains to Barry's parents who go to his pediatrician. The pediatrician is likely to prescribe a drug for Barry,
    a. diazepam (Valium).
    b. methylphenidate (Ritalin).
    c. lithium carbonate.
    d. chlorpromazine (Thorazine).

14. The reported success of megavitamin therapy and the orthomolecular approach is probably due to the
    a. relief of synaptic pathway blockages.
    b. blockage of norepinephrine at neural transmitter sites.
    c. increase of seritonin level in the bloodstream.
    d. placebo effect.

15. Hemodialysis therapy is a recent approach to the treatment of
    a. bipolar affective psychosis.
    b. anxiety.
    c. schizophrenia.
    d. depression.

17
Psychologically based therapies

OVERVIEW

This chapter describes in some detail what mental health professionals do about all the types of problems discussed in the earlier chapters. There are a wide variety of techniques available, and often completely different approaches have been developed for the same problem behavior. These various approaches to treatment are all outgrowths of the different models of psychopathology described earlier. This material is confusing at first because of the natural tendency to feel that one approach must be right and the others wrong. In reality, no general approach to psychotherapy has proved capable of handling the wide range of problems seen clinically. Consequently, the tendency to identify strongly with one approach or another is decreasing. Today, many therapists are familiar with a variety of techniques chosen from several theapeutic approaches and use them depending on the type of problems the client is having. Some therapists, however, prefer to use only one type of treatment. In this case, they try to develop a professional reputation as a certain type of therapist so that only clients appropriate to their chosen orientation are referred to them.

TERMS YOU SHOULD KNOW

psychotherapy (p. 630)

"YAVIS" phenomenon (p. 632)

physician (p. 632)

clergy (p. 632)

psychiatrist (p. 633)

clinical psychologist (p. 633)

psychiatric social worker (p. 633)

token economics (p. 645)

behavioral contracting (pp. 646–647)

assertiveness therapy (p. 647)

assertiveness treatment (p. 647)

biofeedback (p. 648)

thermistors (p. 649)

coverants (p. 650)

cognitive-behavioral therapy (p. 650)

rational-emotive therapy (RET) (p. 651)

cognitive behavioral therapy for depression (p. 652)

stress-inoculation training (p. 654)

client-centered therapy (p. 656)

humanistic-experiential therapy (p. 656)

client-centered (or person-centered or nondirective) therapy (p. 656)

existential psychotherapy (p. 659)

Gestalt therapy (p. 660)

couple counseling (marital therapy) (p. 662)

family therapy (p. 663)

structured family therapy (p. 664)

child (ego state) (p. 665)

parent (ego state) (p. 665)

adult (ego state) (p. 665)

(contingencies) (p. 666)

(conflict resolution) (p. 666)

(contingency contracting) (p. 666)

CONCEPTS TO MASTER

1. Introduction
   a. Psychotherapy is based on the *assumption* that even in cases where physical pathology is present, changes in _____ will have to occur if recovery is to take place. The belief that individuals can _____ is the underlying assumption of all psychotherapy approaches. (p. 630)

b. There are six general goals of psychotherapy. Following are four of the goals; fill in the missing two. (p. 630)
   1. changing maladaptive behavior
   2. changing environmental conditions that may be causing or maintaining the maladaptive behavior
   3. improving interpersonal skills
   4. resolving inner conflicts.
   5.

   6.

2. An overview of psychological treatment
   All psychotherapies share an orientation that is directed toward _____
   and all psychotherapies involve _____. (p. 631)
3. Who receives psychotherapy
   a. Describe the obvious clients for psychotherapy. (p. 631)

   b. What types of individuals are likely to be reluctant clients? (p. 631)

   c. Clients who do the best in psychotherapy are often "YAVIS" types. Explain this statement. (p. 632)

4. Who provides psychotherapeutic services
   a. Fill in the blank spaces in the following chart that summarizes the training and special duties of the professionals on the mental health team.

Professional	Training	Special Duties
psychiatrist (p. 633)	MD degree plus three-year residency of hospital	
clinical psychologist (p. 633)		
psychiatric social worker (p. 633)	BA and MA in social sciences	family evaluation

5. The therapeutic relationship
   a. What is the patient's major contribution to the therapeutic relationship?   (p. 634)

   b. The patient's "expectation of receiving help" is also important to the outcome of therapy and may operate to some degree as a placebo does in medicine. Explain this statement.   (p. 635)

   c. Are a therapist's personality characteristics directly related to the outcome of therapy?   (p. 635)

6. Psychodynamic therapy
   a. Psychodynamic therapy is a treatment approach that emphasizes
   _____.   (p. 635)

   b. There are four basic techniques of psychoanalysis: free association, dream interpretation, analysis of resistance, and analysis of transference. Briefly explain how the analyst uses each technique.
      1. free association   (p. 636)

      2. dream interpretation   (p. 636)

      3. analysis of resistance   (p. 637)

4. analysis of transference. (p. 637)

c. How do most modern analysts like Mann and Strupp differ in emphasis from strict Freudian psychoanalysis? (p. 639)

7. Evaluation of psychodynamic therapy
   a. Indicate whether each of the following statements represents a valid criticism of psychodynamic therapy. Circle the correct response. (p. 640)
      1. It's time consuming and expensive. True False
      2. It's based on a questionable theory of human nature. True False
      3. It neglects the patient's current problems. True False
      4. There is inadequate proof of its effectiveness. True False
   b. For whom is psychodynamic therapy the treatment to choose? (p. 640)

8. Behavioral therapy
   a. How is the maladjusted person seen as differing from the adjusted person in the behavioristic perspective? (p. 640)

   b. The behavioristic perspective views the maladjusted person as one who has
      1. failed to acquire compentencies, or
      2. learned faulty coping.
      Instead of exploring past traumatic events or inner conflicts, behavior therapists manipulate environmental contingencies to alter maladaptive behavior.
      Fill in the requested information in the following chart that summarizes several of the commonly used behavioral therapy techniques.

Behavioral Therapy Technique	Description
1. simple extinction	a. This technique is based on the observation that learned behavior patterns weaken over time if not _____. (p. 641) b. It works best on behavior that is being _____ _____ reinforced. (p. 641)
2. implosive therapy and flooding	a. These techniques rely on the principle of _____. (p. 641) b. With implosion, the problematic behavior is removed by the therapist deliberately trying to _____ anxiety rather than to minimize it. (p. 641) c. What techniques can be used with patients who are not able to realistically imagine scenes? (p. 641) d. Which technique is more effective: implosion, in vivo or flooding in imagination? e. What unfavorable results have been reported from implosion therapy? (p. 642)
3. systematic desensitization	a. The technique is designed to eliminate behaviors that are being _____ reinforced but can be used for other types of problems. (p. 642) b. The procedure consists of three steps. What are they? (p. 642) 　1. 　2. 　3. c. The procedure doesn't work well with the following types of clients: (p. 643)
4. aversion	a. This approach involves modification of behavior by _____ which can be of two types. These two types are: (p. 644) 　1. 　2.

	b. The use of electric shock as an aversive stimulus has decreased recently because of what two reasons? (p. 644) 1. 2. What method is often used instead by clinicians such as Lovaas? (p. 644)
5. modeling	a. Modeling involves learning skills through _____. (p. 645) b. Modeling may be used in clinical situations such as _____. (p. 645)
6. systematic uses of positive reinforcement	a. Briefly describe each of the following techniques: 1. response shaping (p. 645) 2. token economy. (p. 645) b. What are the goals of a token economy program? (pp. 645–646)
7. behavioral contracting	a. A behavioral contract often specifies _____ as well as the responsibilities of the other person to provide tangible rewards in return. (p. 647) b. Briefly list some of the ways a behavioral contract can facilitate therapy. (p. 647)
8. assertiveness training	a. Assertiveness is used both as a method of _____ and as a means of teaching more effective coping techniques. (p. 647) b. Assertiveness training works because each act of intentional assertion inhibits the _____ associated with the situation. (p. 647)
9. biofeedback training	a. Biofeedback consists of three steps. What are they? (p. 648) 1. 2. 3.

	b.	Biofeedback is commonly used on the following types of problems: (p. 648)
	c.	Is there unequivocal data supporting the effectiveness of biofeedback with conditions such as migraine headaches? (p. 649)
	d.	How does the effectiveness of biofeedback (which requires expensive machinery) compare to the effectiveness of relaxation training (which requires next to no special equipment)? (p. 649)

10. Cognitive-behavioral therapy
  a. How have behavioral therapists recently changed their thinking so that many are now labeled "cognitive-behavioral therapists"? (p. 650)

  b. At present, there are several alternative approaches to cognitive-behavioral therapy, but two main themes seem to characterize them all. What are these two themes? (p. 650)
     1.

     2.

  c . The chart below summarizes three different cognitive-behavioral therapies. Fill in the requested information.

Therapeutic Approach	Description
1. rational-emotive therapy (RET)	a. This approach was developed by _____. Today, it is one of the most widely used therapeutic approaches. (p. 651) b. Why does Ellis believe that many of us behave irrationally and feel unnecessarily that we are failures? (p. 651) How have Arnhoff and Glass (1982) criticized this viewpoint? (p. 651)

		c. To change this situation, the RET therapist disputes these false beliefs through _____ and brings about changed thoughts and behaviors through the use of _____ techniques. (p. 652)
2.	cognitive-behavioral therapy for depression	a. This therapy was developed by _____ for the treatment of _____. (p. 652) b. A basic assumption of this approach is that problems like depression result from a person's negative views about himself or herself, the world, and the future. Such behavior typically includes features such as the following. Briefly describe each one: (p. 652) 1. selective perception 2. overgeneralization 3. magnification 4. absolutistic thinking. c. Describe how Beck's approach to changing irrational thinking differs from Ellis's RET. (p. 652) d. Cognitive restructuring may involve other techniques as well. Briefly describe each one: (pp. 652–654) 1. schedule of daily activities 2. discovery of automatic thoughts.
3.	stress-inoculation training	a. This approach was developed by _____. (p. 654) b. Stress-inoculation training usually involves three stages. Briefly describe what happens at each of the stages: (pp. 654–655) 1. cognitive preparation 2. skill acquisition and rehearsal 3. application and practice. c. This approach has been successfully employed in the following cases: (p. 656) It is particularly suited to increasing the adaptive capacities of individuals who have shown a vulnerability to: (p. 656)

11. Evaluation of cognitive-behavioral therapy
    a. Indicate whether each of the following statements is true or false by circling the appropriate response. (p. 656)

Data on RET and cognitive therapy for depression indicate they are successful in promoting change.   True   False

There are questions whether cognitive-behavioral therapy is really "behavioral."   True   False

12. Humanistic-experiential therapies
   a. These approaches have developed in reaction to behavioral and psychodynamic therapies which are believed to fail to accurately account for

   _____.   (p. 656)

   b. Humanistic-experiential therapies are based on a major assumption. What is it?   (p. 656)

   How do behavioral therapists differ from humanistic therapists on this assumption?   (p. 656)

   c. The chart below summarizes the major approaches to psychotherapy that are humanistic-experiential oriented. Fill in the requested information.

Therapeutic Approach	Description
1. client-centered (nondirective) therapy	a. This therapy was originated by _____ in the 1940s as an alternative to psychoanalysis. In this therapy, the psychoanalytic view of humans as irrational and the idea that the proper role of the therapist is to be the director of therapy are rejected. (p. 656) b. The primary role of client-centered therapy is to remove "incongruence." What is incongruence and how does it come about? , (p. 658) How does the client-centered therapist remove incongruence? (p. 658) c. "Pure" client-centered therapy is rarely used today, but it has been influential. How are the experiential therapies of today similar to client-centered therapy, and how are they different? (pp. 658–659)
2. existential therapy	a. Existential therapists do not follow any rigidly prescribed procedures, but they all emphasize the _____ of each individual. (p. 659)

<table>
<tr><td></td><td>b.</td><td>In contrast to the behavioral therapist, the existential therapist _____ his or her feelings and values with the client.   (p. 659)</td></tr>
<tr><td></td><td>c.</td><td>For what types of clients is this therapy indicated?   (p. 659)</td></tr>
<tr><td>3. Gestalt therapy</td><td>a.</td><td>This therapy was originated by _____ as a means of teaching clients to recognize _____ and emotional modalities that they had been _____.   (p. 660)</td></tr>
<tr><td></td><td>b.</td><td>The main goal of Gestalt therapy is to increase _____.   (p. 660)</td></tr>
<tr><td></td><td>c.</td><td>Gestalt therapy sessions focus on the more obvious elements of a person's behavior; thus the sessions are often called _____ training.   (p. 661)</td></tr>
<tr><td></td><td>d.</td><td>What is "taking care of unfinished business"?   (p. 661)</td></tr>
<tr><td></td><td>e.</td><td>Gestalt therapy is said to have become widely used because it blends many of the strong points of psychoanalysis, behavioral therapy, and humanistic-existential therapy. Indicate what Gestalt therapy shares with each of these therapies.   (p. 661)</td></tr>
</table>

13. Evaluation of the humanistic-experiential therapies
    a. There are three major criticisms that have been made of humanistic-experiential therapies. What are they?   (p. 661)
        1.

        2.

        3.

14. Therapy for interpersonal relationships
    a. These therapeutic techniques focus on relationships rather than individuals and emphasize the role of faulty communication in causing maladaptive behavior.   (p. 662)
        The following chart summarizes the major forms of interpersonal therapy. Fill in the missing information.

Therapeutic Approach	Description
1. couple counseling (marital therapy)	a. Can improvements in marital relationships usually be accomplished by undertaking therapy with one member but not the other? (p. 662) b. How do happily married couples differ from unhappily married couples? (p. 662) c. How are videotapes useful in couple counseling? (p. 662) d. How effective are marital therapies at resolving crisis according to Cookery (1980)? (p. 663)
2. family therapy	a. How did family therapy originate? (p. 663) b. Who does the family therapist view as the "patient" in family therapy? (p. 663) c. The most widely used approach to family therapy is _____ developed by Satir (1967). This therapy emphasizes improving family communication and interactions. (p. 663) d. Another approach is called "structured family therapy" and was developed by _____. This therapy assumes that if the family context changes, then the individual members will change. Thus, an important goal is to change the family organization so that family members will behave: (p. 664) Structured therapy has been used successfully with: (pp. 664–665) e. Which approach to family therapy has been found to be most effective (Gurman and Kniskern (1978)? (p. 665) f. How does the success of family therapy compare to individual therapy? (p. 665)

3. transactional analysis	a. What happens if one party stops playing a game? (p. 665)
	b. Describe each of the following games people may play:
	  1. "Why don't you—yes but" (pp. 666–667)
	  2. "wooden leg" (p. 667)
	  3. "Now I've got you, you son of a bitch." (p. 667)
	c. What is the purpose of analyzing the "games" people play? (p. 667)

15. Integration of therapy approaches
    a. What have psychodynamic therapists had to acknowledge about behavioral techniques?   (p. 667)

    b. What have behavioral therapists had to acknowledge about relationship factors?   (p. 667)

    c. Kendall (1982) has summarized the reasons there is interest in integrating the approaches to psychotherapy, but he has also noted the obstacles to integration. Summarize these arguments below.   (p. 668)

    Reason for Integration   Obstacles to Integration of
    of Therapeutic Approaches   Therapeutic Approaches
    1.   1.

    2.   2.

    3.   3.

    4.

16. Evaluation of success in psychotherapy
    a. The chart below lists some of the sources of information that can be used to gauge the outcome of psychotherapy and also note the bias inherent in each source. Fill in missing information.

Source	Bias
1. therapist	Wants to see him/herself as competent and successful.
2. patient (pp. 668–669)	
3. (p. 669)	May tend to see what they want to see but are often more realistic than therapist or client.

b. The rate of improvement in most studies of therapy outcome regardless of approach is
_____ percent.   (p. 669)

(17.) Descriptive comparison of various approaches to psychotherapy
Place a symbol along each of the following continua to indicate the position of each therapeutic
approach.   (pp. 636–637)

△ **psychodynamic**
□ **behavioral**
< **cognitive-behavioral**
* **humanistic-existential**
○ **interactional**

△
Individual _____ **Group**

                △
Cognitive _____ **Behavior**
change   **change**

                        △
Directive _____ **Nondirective**

        △
Inner control _____ **Outer control**
of behavior   **of behavior**

        △
Historical _____ **Here and now**
focus   **focus**

                                                  △
Brief _____ **Long term**

(18.) The use of hypnosis in therapy
    a.   Describe how a hypnotic trance is induced.   (p. 638)

    b.   Hypnosis may be used to accomplish the following outcomes. Briefly describe what each
one is: (pp. 638–639)
        1.   recall of buried memories

        2.   age regression

        3.   dream induction

        4.   post-hypnotic suggestion.

    c.   Is there any evidence that hypnosis really works for anything?   (p. 639)

    d.   How might drugs sometimes be used in the hypnotic procedure?   (p. 639)

(19.) Group therapy
What school of psychotherapy does group therapy follow?   (p. 657)

(20.) Structured behavioral therapy for couples
Weiss (1975) has developed a brief, highly structured form of couple therapy. Briefly describe the
major things he tries to teach couples.   (p. 666)

CHAPTER QUIZ

1. Which of the following clients is most likely to demonstrate the "YAVIS" phenomenon?
   a. A reluctant alcoholic client whose spouse threatens "therapy or get out."
   b. A person suffering long-term psychological distress.
   c. A comparatively normal person who enters therapy out of a sense he or she has not lived up to his or her own expectations.
   d. A case where physical pathology is present.

2. The member of the mental health team who has specialization in personality theory, psychological assessment, and psychotherapy is a
   a. psychiatrist.
   b. clinical psychologist.
   c. psychiatric social worker.
   d. pastoral counselor.

3. The patient's major contribution to the therapeutic relationship is his/her
   a. motivation.
   b. financial incentives for therapist.
   c. expectation of receiving help.
   d. suggestibility.

4. A male employee is physically attracted to his female boss, but he is not consciously aware of his attraction. The night before they are to make a business trip, he dreams their plane crashes and they are marooned alone together on a desert island. Freud would label the desert island story the _____ content of the dream.
   a. manifest
   b. sublimated
   c. condensed
   d. latent

5. A son of a critical father comes to therapy one day and with no provocation is extremely hostile in his remarks to the therapist. The therapist might consider that _____ is occurring.
   a. free association
   b. countertransference
   c. transference
   d. positive transference

6. Contemporary psychodynamic treatment differs from Freudian psychoanalysis by placing more emphasis on
   a. early repressed sexuality.
   b. current ego functioning.
   c. long-term treatment.
   d. childhood events.

7. Instructing a woman with fear of water to imagine taking a bath in a bottomless tub is an example of
   a. implosion.
   b. flooding.
   c. in vivo techniques.
   d. desensitization.

8. After a patient has been trained in relaxation, the next step in the desensitization procedure is
   a. construction of hierarchies.
   b. a marathon desensitization group.
   c. to use a tape recorder to carry out desensitization at home.
   d. for the client to remain relaxed and imagine scenes.
9. Desensitization is particularly effective with
   a. examination anxiety, phobias, anxiety disorders.
   b. severely disturbed autistic children.
   c. mentally retarded adults.
   d. problems with open expression of thoughts and feelings.
10. A patient is exposed to behaviors or roles in peers or therapists and encouraged to imitate the new behaviors. This therapeutic technique is called
    a. response shaping.
    b. modeling.
    c. assertiveness training.
    d. behavioral contracting.
11. Which of the following statements regarding biofeedback is true?
    a. Biofeedback is a more elaborate means of teaching relaxation.
    b. Biofeedback is more effective than relaxation training.
    c. The effects of biofeedback are often generalized outside the laboratory.
    d. Recent well-controlled studies of biofeedback have shown a treatment effect for migraine patients.
12. According to Aaron Beck (1979), individuals maintain false beliefs even in the face of contradictory evidence because
    a. they are reinforced for doing so.
    b. of biologically based drives to do so.
    c. of a strong regressive pull to be a "child" or a "parent" rather than an "adult."
    d. they engage in selective perception and overgeneralization.
13. Which therapy consists of these three stages: cognitive preparation, skill acquisition and rehearsal, application and practice.
    a. RET
    b. cognitive therapy for depression
    c. stress innoculation therapy
    d. assertiveness therapy
14. Among couples who underwent marital therapy together, Cookery (1980) reported _____ percent stayed married.
    a. 50 percent
    b. 29 percent
    c. 15 percent
    d. 5 percent
15. The rate of improvement given in most studies of psychotherapy outcome is between _____ percent regardless of method.
    a. 50–60
    b. 60–70
    c. 70–80
    d. 80–90.

18

Contemporary issues in abnormal psychology

OVERVIEW

Previous chapters have catalogued the many forms of mental disorders and have briefly described various treatment programs, most of which focus either directly on the patient or involve only immediate family measures. The focus of Chapter 18 is different. The chapter introduces the idea of "primary prevention" that emphasizes programs and research at the level of the broader society in order to prevent maladaptive behavior in the first place. Thus, the focus of this chapter differs in two ways from earlier ones. First, it discusses interventions at the broader societal level and second, it emphasizes prevention rather than treatment. The chapter discusses how the U.S. government is involved both nationally and internationally in improving mental health. The chapter also addresses controversial legal issues. Many people were shocked when John Hinkley was found not guilty of shooting President Ronald Reagan, especially since we all saw him do the shooting right on television. The chapter attempts to describe the maze of laws pertaining to the insanity defense and other pertinent legal issues.

TERMS YOU SHOULD KNOW

primary prevention (p. 674)

secondary prevention (p. 674)

tertiary prevention (p. 674)

epidemiological studies (p. 677)

crisis intervention (p. 677)

short-term crisis therapy (p. 677)

257

258

(right to treatment) (p. 684)

(freedom from custodial confinement) (p. 684)

(right to compensation) (p. 684)

(right to legal counsel) (p. 684)

(right to live in the community) (p. 684)

(right to refuse treatment) (p. 684)

(right to less restrictive treatment) (p. 684)

CONCEPTS TO MASTER

1. Introduction
   Why are funds targeted for prevention programs likely to be cut during periods of economic conservatism and restraint?   (p. 673)

2. Primary prevention
   a. Primary prevention involves research into the conditions that foster mental disorders. Primary prevention also involves the eradication of negative conditions and institution of circumstances that foster mental health. Fill in the missing information on the following chart that illustrates various primary prevention measures.

Primary Prevention Measures	
1. biological (p. 674)	Examples of biological prevention include:
2. psychosocial (p. 674)	Examples of psychosocial prevention include preparation for:
3. sociocultural (p. 675)	Sociocultural prevention is focused on making the _____ as "nourishing" as possible. Examples of sociocultural prevention include:

3. Secondary prevention
   a. Epidemiological studies
      Secondary prevention emphasizes early identification and treatment of maladaptive behavior before it can become seriously disabling. How do epidemiological studies assist in secondary prevention? (p. 677)

   b. Crisis intervention
      Crisis intervention is an attempt at secondary prevention that aims at delivering prompt treatment. In what ways are prompt services given? (p. 677)
      1.

      2.

      What is the sole concern of short-term crisis therapy? How long does such therapy last? (p. 677)

      Why is crisis intervention discouraging for the therapist? (p. 678)

   c. Consultation and education
      What does "consultation and education of intermediaries" mean? (p. 678)

   d. Therapeutic community
      Describe the following aspects of a therapeutic community. (p. 678)
      1. staff expectations

      2. do-it-yourself attitude.

      A persistent danger with hospitalization is that the hospital will become a permanent refuge. To keep the focus on returning the patient to the community and on preventing the disorder from becoming chronic, hospital staffs try to establish _____ and to maintain a _____ attitude. (p. 679)

Between _____ and _____ percent of patients treated this way can be discharged within a few weeks or at most a few months. (p. 679)

e. Lentz (1977) performed an evaluation of the relative effectiveness of three treatment approaches for chronic hospitalized patients.

   1. Describe the three treatments that were compared. (p. 679)

     1.

     2.

     3.

   2. Describe how the study was carried out. (pp. 679–680)

   3. Who were the subjects?

   4. What were the results of the study? (p. 680)

4. Tertiary prevention

   a. Many studies have found that as many as _____ percent of schizophrenic patients have been rehospitalized within one year of their discharge. Aftercare programs reduce the rehospitalization. Describe the following aftercare programs:

     1. halfway house (p. 681)

     2. day hospitals. (p. 681)

b. Does adequate aftercare reduce the chances of rehospitalization, according to Glass-cote (1978)? (p. 681)

c. Fairweather et al. (1969) studied patients who had been placed in a halfway house and compared them to patients who had not had halfway house experience. How did the two groups differ? (p. 681)

5. The commitment process

In most cases people are sent to state mental hospitals voluntarily. However, there are four conditions on which a person can be formally committed. They are (p. 683)

1.

2.

3.

4.

Commitment is a civil court proceeding that varies slightly from state to state. Describe a typical procedure. (p. 683)

6. Assessment of "dangerousness"

a. How many individuals did Rubin (1972) state are confined because they are dangerous? (p. 685)
1. In state mental hospitals _____.
2. In prisons _____.

b. Why are violent acts particularly dangerous to predict? (p. 685)

c. When assessing dangerousness, psychological testing usually focuses on

_____. (p. 686)

7. Duty-to-warn: implications of the Tarasoff decision
   a. When does a clinician have a "duty-to-warn?"

   b. Does the doctrine extend to suicidal cases?

8. The insanity plea
   a. How frequently is the insanity plea used?

   b. How does the time served by the criminal sent to a psychiatric hospital compare to time served by criminals sent to prison?

   c. What does the verdict "guilty but mentally ill" mean? Is it a good idea?

9. Deinstitutionalization
   a. Sice 1955 what has happened to the number of persons hospitalized in state mental hospitals? What accounts for the changes?

   b. What unforseen problems have arisen in the effort to deinstitutionalize the mentally ill?

   c. How much street cime in New York is attributed to released mental patients?

   d. Describe the chronic social breakdown syndrome.

e.   Bachrach (1980) has developed a program to reintegrate chronic mental patients into the community. Of what elements does it consist?   (pp. 690–691)

f.   Short-term rehospitalization is not viewed as a failure of deinstitutionalization. Why not?   (p. 691)

10. Organized efforts for mental health
     a.   The extent of mental disorders was brought to public attention during World War II. How?   (p. 691)

     b.   Following is a diagram of the government's mental health departments. Fill in the missing information.   (p. 692)

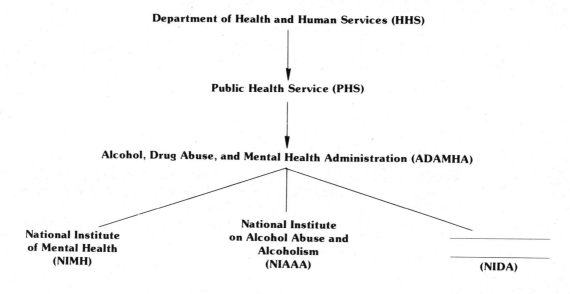

     c.   What type of activities does the NIMH do?   (p. 692)

     d.   Does the federal government directly supervise local community services?   (p. 692)

State hospitals? (p. 692)

What has happened to these programs in recent years? (p. 692)

e. What are the three purposes of a professional organization such as the American Psychological Association? (pp. 692–693)
   1.

   2.

   3.

f. What is the role of voluntary groups in regard to mental health needs? (p. 693)

g. Private industries also have a role in mental health services. Describe how the Control Data Corporation meets employees mental health needs. (pp. 694–695)

11. International efforts for mental health
   a. It has been estimated that over _____ million people worldwide are affected by alcoholism, drug abuse, mental retardation, organic brain disorders, and mental disorders. (The population of the United States is only around 220 million.) (p. 696)
   b. Briefly describe the efforts of the following international organizations to improve mental health:
      1. World Health Organization (WHO) (p. 696)

      2. United Nations Educational, Scientific, and Cultural Organization (UNESCO). (p. 696)

12. The individual contribution
   Indicate whether each of the following is true or false by circling the appropriate response. (p. 700)

1. From time to time, *everyone* has serious difficulty coping with problems.   True   False
2. During such a crisis, professional assistance may be needed.   True   False
3. Such difficulties can happen to *anyone* if the stress is severe.   True   False
4. Early detection and treatment is important to prevent chronic conditions.   True   False

(13.) The hospitalization syndrome
     a.   Describe the elements of the social breakdown syndrome.   (p. 682)
         1.   deficiency in self-concept

         2.   social labeling

         3.   the sick role

         4.   atrophy of work and social skills

         5.   development of chronic sick roles.

     b.   Are characteristics of the patient thought to interact with the hospital milieu in formation of the social breakdown syndrome?   (p. 682)

CHAPTER QUIZ

1. All of the following are examples of primary prevention *except*
     a.   professional athletes who talk about their own difficulties.
     b.   genetic counseling.
     c.   the prison system.
     d.   nationalized health care.
2. Epidemiological studies are important in
     a.   determining which persons would benefit from long-term, as opposed to short-term, treatment.
     b.   evaluating the effect of an interdisciplinary approach to treatment of maladaptive behaviors.
     c.   the early detection and prompt treatment of maladaptive behaviors.
     d.   assessing the public's attitude toward mental health programs.

3. Allen Jones is a middle-aged factory worker, husband, and father of five children. He has never previously been involved in psychotherapy until his home is destroyed in a tornado. While he attempts to find housing for his family, he discovers that his wife wants a divorce. He immediately becomes quite depressed and is unable to follow through on his house-seeking. Allen Jones is a prime candidate for
    a. day hospitalization.
    b. crisis intervention.
    c. psychoanalysis.
    d. milieu therapy.
4. The approach that should be taken for Allen Jones from Question 3 would be an example of
    a. secondary prevention.
    b. primary prevention.
    c. epidemiological intervention.
    d. tertiary prevention.
5. The purpose of consultation work by community mental health professionals is
    a. crisis intervention.
    b. to reach individuals in need of help who would otherwise never be identified by any community agency.
    c. tertiary prevention.
    d. to reach a larger group of persons in need by working with intermediary agents.
6. Milieu therapy is
    a. the temporary substitution of one treatment mode by another until adequate resources can be acquired to provide the treatment of chioce.
    b. a general term for any form of preventive treatment.
    c. the establishment of a hospital environment itself as a therapeutic community.
    d. the integration of any two distinct forms of treatment.
7. Which of the following is a growing trend in the treatment modes used in mental hospitals today?
    a. Establishment of the hospital environment itself as a therapeutic community.
    b. Emphasis on a "private practice model" with decisions made by a single physician.
    c. Long-term hospitalization, even for first admissions, in an effort to prevent rehospitalization.
    d. Integration of mental patients with other somatic patients on hospital wards.
8. A person may be committed involuntarily by a civil proceeding on all the following grounds *except*
    a. dangerous to him or herself or to others.
    b. senile.
    c. unable to make decisions.
    d. incapable of providing for his or her basic physical needs.
9. The duty-to-warn doctrine refers to a psychologist's responsibility to
    a. warn the police if a client has revealed a criminal act.
    b. warn the IRS if a client isn't paying taxes.
    c. tell parents when a minor child seeks therapy.
    d. tell a person that a client has made threats on his or her life.
10. The _____ rule suggests that a defendant should be found innocent if his/her act was a "product of mental disease or defect."
    a. M'Naughton
    b. irresistible impulse
    c. Durham
    d. diminished capacity.

11. All of the following are false beliefs on which the policy of deinstitutionalization was based *except*
    a. all mental health problems can be managed with medication.
    b. society wants and will finance community-based care.
    c. community-based services are more economical than state hospitals.
    d. many residents of institutions have no homes or relatives to go to.
12. In New York City _____ percent of street crime is attributable to former psychiatric patients.
    a. 20
    b. 40
    c. 60
    d. 80.
13. Programs to prevent chronic social breakdown involve all the following *except*
    a. standard treatment plans for case management.
    b. hospital liaison.
    c. trained staff.
    d. targeting of chronic patients.
14. Which of the following statements regarding trends in psychiatric hospitalization is *false?*
    a. Populations in state mental hospitals have dramatically increased.
    b. The number of hospital admissions has increased significantly.
    c. Hospitalizations are briefer and more frequent.
    d. Half of released patients are readmitted within a year.
15. An international agency interested in mental health concerns is
    a. APA.
    b. NIMH.
    c. WHO.
    d. NIDA.

ANSWER KEY

Chapter 1   ABNORMAL BEHAVIOR IN OUR TIMES

1. c (p. 5)	6. b (p. 16)	11. b (p. 18)
2. d (pp. 10–14)	7. c (p. 16)	12. d (p. 21)
3. d (p. 12 & 13)	8. a (p. 17)	13. b (p. 24)
4. b (p. 15)	9. d (p. 19)	14. c (p. 25)
5. c (p. 15)	10. a (p. 18)	15. c (p. 26)

Chapter 2   HISTORICAL VIEWS OF ABNORMAL BEHAVIOR

1. a (p. 31)	6. d (p. 36)	11. a (pp. 46 & 47)
2. d (pp. 32 & 33)	7. b (p. 41)	12. d (p. 49)
3. a (p. 33)	8. c (p. 43)	13. c (p. 49)
4. d (p. 34)	9. c (pp. 43 & 44)	14. c (p. 49)
5. b (p. 34)	10. a (p. 46)	15. d (p. 53)

Chapter 3   BIOLOGICAL, PSYCHOSOCIAL, AND SOCIOCULTURAL VIEWPOINTS

1. a (p. 58)	6. b (p. 63)	11. d (p. 73)
2. b (p. 58)	7. c (p. 66)	12. d (p. 75)
3. d (pp. 58–60)	8. b (pp. 67 & 68)	13. a (p. 76)
4. c (pp. 60–62)	9. b (p. 70)	14. b (p. 88)
5. a (p. 63)	10. d (p. 72)	15. d (p. 90)

Chapter 4   CAUSAL FACTORS IN ABNORMAL BEHAVIOR

1. c (p. 94)	6. a (p. 105)	11. a (p. 116)
2. a (p. 95)	7. d (p. 106)	12. c (p. 120)
3. b (p. 98)	8. c (pp. 106 & 108)	13. c (p. 122)
4. d (p. 101)	9. b (p. 110)	14. d (p. 124)
5. b (p. 104)	10. d (pp. 111 & 112)	15. a (p. 129)

Chapter 5   STRESS AND ADJUSTMENT DISORDERS

1. b (p. 142)	6. b (p. 152)	11. a (p. 159)
2. b (p. 143)	7. d (p. 153)	12. c (p. 163)
3. c (pp. 145 & 146)	8. b (p. 153)	13. d (p. 167)
4. d (p. 147)	9. a (p. 155)	14. d (p. 170)
5. c (pp. 148 & 149)	10. b (p. 157)	15. c (p. 178)

Chapter 6   ANXIETY-BASED DISORDERS (NEUROSES)

1. c (p. 188)	6. b (p. 207)	11. b (p. 219)
2. a (p. 192)	7. b (p. 215)	12. d (p. 223)
3. c (p. 195)	8. c (p. 215)	13. a (p. 224)
4. b (pp. 199 & 202)	9. d (p. 216)	14. b (p. 225)
5. a (pp. 204 & 205)	10. c (p. 217)	15. c (p. 227)

Chapter 7   PERSONALITY DISORDERS AND CRIME

1. d (p. 233)	6. a (p. 244)	11. a (p. 249)
2. b (p. 235)	7. d (p. 244)	12. c (p. 253)
3. c (p. 235)	8. d (p. 245)	13. a (p. 254)
4. a (p. 237)	9. a (p. 246)	14. d (p. 258)
5. b (p. 239)	10. d (p. 248)	15. d (p. 260)

Chapter 8   PSYCHOLOGICAL FACTORS AND PHYSICAL ILLNESS

1. d (p. 273)	6. a (p. 277)	11. b (p. 286)
2. b (p. 275)	7. d (p. 279)	12. a (p. 287)
3. d (p. 276)	8. b (p. 280)	13. a (p. 288)
4. c (p. 276)	9. d (p. 281)	14. a (p. 290)
5. c (p. 277)	10. c (p. 282)	15. a (p. 291)

Chapter 9   AFFECTIVE DISORDERS AND SUICIDE

1. a (p. 303)	6. b (p. 314)	11. a (p. 326)
2. c (p. 304)	7. d (p. 315)	12. a (p. 329)
3. d (p. 308)	8. c (p. 318)	13. d (p. 331)
4. d (p. 309)	9. b (p. 319)	14. a (p. 332)
5. b (p. 311)	10. b (p. 324)	15. a (p. 333)

Chapter 10   SCHIZOPHRENIC DISORDERS AND PARANOIA

1. c.(p. 343)	6. a (p. 351)	11. c (p. 368)
2. b (p. 345)	7. a (p. 354)	12. d (p. 373)
3. b (p. 345)	8. b (p. 356)	13. c (p. 375)
4. c (p. 349)	9. a (p. 359)	14. c (p. 380)
5. d (p. 350)	10. d (p. 367)	15. b (p. 385)

Chapter 11   SUBSTANCE-USE AND OTHER ADDICTIVE DISORDERS

1. a (p. 397)	6. a (p. 407)	11. b (p. 414)
2. d (p. 400)	7. c (p. 407)	12. d (p. 417)
3. d (p. 403)	8. d (p. 409)	13. c (p. 431)
4. b (p. 405)	9. c (p. 411)	14. d (p. 426)
5. a (p. 404)	10. c (p. 414)	15. c (p. 439)

Chapter 12   PSYCHOSEXUAL DISORDERS AND VARIANTS

1. b (p. 451)	6. b (p. 459)	11. b (p. 465)
2. a (p. 451)	7. d (p. 460)	12. a (p. 475)
3. a (p. 453)	8. b (p. 462)	13. a (p. 476)
4. d (p. 457)	9. c (p. 464)	14. b (p. 479)
5. d (p. 457)	10. a (p. 464)	15. c (p. 481)

Chapter 13   ORGANIC MENTAL DISORDERS AND MENTAL RETARDATION

1. a (p. 489)	6. a (p. 497)	11. a (p. 507)
2. b (p. 490)	7. b (pp. 498 & 499)	12. d (p. 517)
3. c (p. 491)	8. c (p. 499)	13. a (p. 518)
4. b (p. 494)	9. b (p. 500)	14. c (p. 522)
5. d (p. 496)	10. a (p. 506)	15. d (p. 526)

Chapter 14   BEHAVIOR DISORDERS OF CHILDHOOD AND ADOLESCENCE

1. b (p. 537)	6. c (p. 550)	11. d (p. 562)
2. d (p. 538)	7. d (p. 552)	12. b (p. 567)
3. d (pp. 539 & 540)	8. b (p. 558)	13. d (p. 572)
4. d (p. 540)	9. c (p. 558)	14. a (p. 573)
5. c (p. 545)	10. a (p. 560)	15. c (p. 576)

Chapter 15   CLINICAL ASSESSMENT

1. c (p. 584)
2. a (p. 585)
3. a (p. 586)
4. c (p. 586)
5. b (p. 590)

6. b (p. 590)
7. b (p. 592)
8. a (p. 593)
9. d (pp. 593 & 594)
10. d (p. 594)

11. d (p. 596)
12. c (p. 596)
13. c (pp. 597 & 598)
14. d (p. 606)
15. b (p. 606)

Chapter 16   BIOLOGICALLY BASED THERAPIES

1. a (p. 611)
2. a (p. 612)
3. c (p. 613)
4. b (p. 613)
5. a (p. 614)

6. c (p. 615)
7. a (p. 616)
8. c (p. 616)
9. d (p. 618)
10. b (p. 620)

11. a (p. 620)
12. c (p. 623)
13. b (p. 624)
14. d (p. 626)
15. c (p. 626)

Chapter 17   PSYCHOLOGICALLY BASED THERAPIES

1. c (p. 632)
2. b (p. 633)
3. a (p. 634)
4. a (p. 636)
5. c (p. 638)

6. b (p. 640)
7. a (p. 641)
8. a (p. 642)
9. a (pp. 643 & 644)
10. b (p. 645)

11. a (p. 649)
12. d (p. 650)
13. c (p. 655)
14. a (p. 663)
15. c (p. 669)

Chapter 18   CONTEMPORARY ISSUES IN ABNORMAL PSYCHOLOGY

1. c (p. 674)
2. c (p. 677)
3. b (p. 677)
4. a (p. 677)
5. d (p. 678)

6. c (p. 678)
7. a (p. 678)
8. b (p. 683)
9. d (p. 686)
10. c (p. 678)

11. d (p. 689)
12. b (p. 690)
13. a (pp. 690 & 691)
14. a (p. 691)
15. c (p. 696)

NOTES

NOTES